IMISCOE Research Series

This series is the official book series of IMISCOE, the largest network of excellence on migration and diversity in the world. It comprises publications which present empirical and theoretical research on different aspects of international migration. The authors are all specialists, and the publications a rich source of information for researchers and others involved in international migration studies. The series is published under the editorial supervision of the IMISCOE Editorial Committee which includes leading scholars from all over Europe. The series, which contains more than eighty titles already, is internationally peer reviewed which ensures that the book published in this series continue to present excellent academic standards and scholarly quality. Most of the books are available open access.

Catherine Wihtol de Wenden

Migration and International Relations

IMISCOE Short Reader

 Springer

Catherine Wihtol de Wenden
Centre de Recherches Internationales
Sciences Po
Paris, France

ISSN 2364-4087   ISSN 2364-4095 (electronic)
IMISCOE Research Series
ISBN 978-3-031-31715-6   ISBN 978-3-031-31716-3 (eBook)
https://doi.org/10.1007/978-3-031-31716-3

This work was supported by IMISCOE

© The Editor(s) (if applicable) and The Author(s) 2023. This book is an open access publication
Open Access This book is licensed under the terms of the Creative Commons Attribution 4.0 International License (http://creativecommons.org/licenses/by/4.0/), which permits use, sharing, adaptation, distribution and reproduction in any medium or format, as long as you give appropriate credit to the original author(s) and the source, provide a link to the Creative Commons license and indicate if changes were made.
The images or other third party material in this book are included in the book's Creative Commons license, unless indicated otherwise in a credit line to the material. If material is not included in the book's Creative Commons license and your intended use is not permitted by statutory regulation or exceeds the permitted use, you will need to obtain permission directly from the copyright holder.
The use of general descriptive names, registered names, trademarks, service marks, etc. in this publication does not imply, even in the absence of a specific statement, that such names are exempt from the relevant protective laws and regulations and therefore free for general use.
The publisher, the authors, and the editors are safe to assume that the advice and information in this book are believed to be true and accurate at the date of publication. Neither the publisher nor the authors or the editors give a warranty, expressed or implied, with respect to the material contained herein or for any errors or omissions that may have been made. The publisher remains neutral with regard to jurisdictional claims in published maps and institutional affiliations.

This Springer imprint is published by the registered company Springer Nature Switzerland AG
The registered company address is: Gewerbestrasse 11, 6330 Cham, Switzerland

Funding Information

This research was funded in whole or in part by the French Agence Nationale de la Recherche (ANR) as part of the project "The Politics of Migration and Asylum Crisis in Europe – PACE" (ANR-18-CE41-0013).

Thanks

We would like to thank Sam Ferguson for his careful work in editing the manuscript of this book.

Introduction

The emergence of migration as a major issue in international relations is a relatively recent phenomenon, since migration was previously studied mainly at the national or local levels, without attention to its connections or interdependency at the global level. For a long time, migration was absent from many international university courses and conferences in international relations, as well as from diplomatic agreements and discussions. Since the 1990s, the importance of migration at the global level has become increasingly apparent, in a large number of domains: refugee crises, the externalisation of borders, the migration-development nexus, the development of migration diplomacy (led by countries of emigration, but with a focus from countries of immigration on border controls, dual citizenship, and multiple allegiances), diasporas and transnationalism, environmentally displaced persons, and finally the emergence of global systems of migration governance with the creation of the Global Forum on Migration and Development (GFMD) and the Marrakech Compact on Migration of 2018, both led by the United Nations. It is therefore apparent that migration has become a central topic of international relations. Public opinion largely fails to recognise the extent to which questions of migration go beyond the level of the state, reducing them instead to more and more localised issues of "living together". However, this vastly increased visibility of migration in both international debate and international mobilisation poses new questions and challenges for the future. This is the central argument of the present work.

How Questions of Migration Bring New Challenges to International Relations

Migration was first studied by sociologists and economists, who focused on its impact on receiving societies, while neglecting the perspective of countries of emigration and the international "soft diplomacy" connected to population movements. Until the 1990s, migration was barely addressed in the field of international relations, except with regard to refugees, and even this was long considered to be a very minor topic. The increasing politicisation of migration policies and mobilisations on the part of migrants, descendants of migrants, and transnational actors, together with the development of comparative studies, led to migration being addressed at other levels of analysis: first at the intersection between the national and the international order, and eventually at the global level. Nonetheless, there remains resistance to seriously addressing questions of migration in many international meetings and conferences.

Migration flows and settlement are increasingly disturbing the paradigm of nation states, challenging their presumed sovereignty over their territory, their laws, and their populations. Nation states often perceive a threat to their prerogatives from the tendency of transnational and international forces to weaken border controls, national identities, and rules governing citizenship – all of which function as classical symbols of power – while promoting cosmopolitanism and an increased role for external actors. Soft diplomacy, manifested in influence, intrusion, or systems of global governance, is gradually replacing state-to-state diplomacy. The growing interdependency between regions in the so-called Global South and Global North is giving a more prominent voice to the former, and bringing new issues onto the international agenda, such as those of environmentally displaced persons, humanitarian problems, and statelessness. The project to construct systems of global migration governance, with the creation of the Global Forum on Migration and Development (GFMD) and the Marrakech Global Compact for Migration (GCM) of 2018, is bringing together actors who were not formerly active in the domain of international relations: IGOs, NGOs, associations, trade unions, churches, experts, and countries of the Global South have all come to play an increasing role in discussions and negotiations.

Citizenship has become an international issue, intersecting with many different domains: notably in countries of immigration, migration raises questions of the granting of citizenship (through naturalisation), dual citizenship, and multiple allegiances, and more broadly of the access of migrants to local political rights. In contexts of rising ethnic identities, common issues include the secularism of the state, religious identities, radicalisation, discrimination, and questions of community-building and exclusion.

In discussions of global migration governance, borders have become the symbol of migration control and management. Such control now uses sophisticated instruments, involving both the internal and the international order, the externalisation of borders into transit countries, and the development of camps and "jungles". It also results in extensive human smuggling, and large numbers of deaths. These phenomena highlight the inequality of citizens across the world with regard to their right to mobility and access to passports. Some of the poorest people in the world are also those who are threatened by environmental disasters (Bangladesh) or statelessness (the Rohingya).

New forms of soft diplomacy are developing, influenced both by immigration and emigration countries, notably relating to border controls and repatriation, and often linked to the negotiation of development policies. Some countries, including

Turkey, Libya, Morocco, and Mexico, have managed to leverage their role as transit countries to gain bargaining power. Some countries harness the power of their diaspora communities in other countries: this can give rise to the paying of remittances, the creation of elite and cultural networks that can support migrant associations in the country of immigration, and control of religious practices abroad. Such practices have led to an increased voice for many of these countries (including Mexico, Turkey, Morocco, Bangladesh, and Nepal) in the global governance of migration, notably in discussions conducted through organisations in the UN System.

The present work provides an international overview of these developments in the place of migration in international relations, drawing on many examples from all over the world, but with a particular focus on the European region. It also adopts a number of different perspectives and theoretical approaches relating to international levels of analysis: the relations between the international and internal orders, and between levels of scale from the local to the global, the changing nature of borders and their externalisation, the roles of diasporas and transnationalism, the failure of nation states in maintaining control of their borders, questions of citizenship, allegiance, and multiculturalism, and finally the development of migration diplomacy.

Contents

1 **International Migration as a World Issue**.................... 1
   1.1 The Globalisation of Migration 2
   1.2 Other Important Developments Over the Last 30 Years 2
      1.2.1 I – The Main Factors Affecting Migration.............. 5
      1.2.2 II – The Various Forms of Mobility................... 6
   1.3 The Impact of the COVID-19 Pandemic: Reinforcing
      the Migration Gap Between North and South 8
      1.3.1 III – Migration in the Euro-Mediterranean Space:
            A Case Study 9
   1.4 Conclusion 13
   References.. 13

2 **Immigration Policies**.. 15
   2.1 Who Is an International Migrant? 16
      2.1.1 I – Literature Review 17
   2.2 Stephen Castles: International Migration
      as a Global Issue 17
   2.3 James Hollifield: The Contemporary Contradictions
      of Economic Liberalism and Security-Based Politics,
      from a Comparative Perspective 18
   2.4 Thomas Faist: The Transnational Social Question
      as an Alternative to Class Struggle at the Global Scale........... 19
   2.5 Aristide Zolberg: "The Main Gate and the Back Door",
      "Strange Bedfellows", and the Influence of External Factors
      on the Internal Political Order 22
      2.5.1 II – Historical Overview 22
   2.6 The Italian Crisis as a Case Study 28
      2.6.1 III – 2015: The Challenge of Asylum for Europe 29

	2.7	Conflict Between EU Member States and EU Institutions	29
	2.8	Factors of Failure and Implications for EU Member States and Institutions	30
	2.9	Civil Society and "Crimes of Solidarity", Ethics Versus Control	32
	2.10	Dilemmas Between Wisdom and Politics: Public Opinion and Decision-Making	32
	2.11	Conclusion	34
		References	34
3	**Refugees**		**37**
	3.1	I – Historical Overview	38
	3.2	II – The Refugee Crisis of 2015: Path Dependency, Crises of Solidarity, and Unanimity Rule in Brussels	40
		3.2.1 The Ukrainian Case: An Exception?	42
	3.3	Conclusion: Is There a Migration Diplomacy Around Refugee Policies?	43
		References	44
4	**Citizenship and Migration in the International Order**		**45**
	4.1	I – Citizenship and Nationality	46
		4.1.1 The French Case: Distinction Between Citizenship and Nationality	47
	4.2	II – Citizenship and Migration in a Globalised World	49
		4.2.1 Citizenship Challenged by Migration	49
		4.2.2 The Multiple Forms of Negotiated Citizenship	52
	4.3	Conclusion	57
		References	57
5	**Migration Diplomacy and Multi-actor Governance**		**59**
	5.1	I – Borders, at the Centre of Migration Diplomacy	60
		5.1.1 Bilateral and Multilateral Agreements	61
	5.2	II – International Conventions and Declarations	62
		5.2.1 Towards an International Governance of Migration	63
	5.3	III – From Local to Global: Cities as New Actors in International Migration	65
		5.3.1 Cities as International Networks	66
		5.3.2 Smart Cities and Cities of Marginalisation	67
		5.3.3 Sanctuary Cities and Welcoming Cities	68
		5.3.4 Cities Are New Actors in Transnational Projects	69
	5.4	Conclusion	71
		References	72

6	**Migration and Development**		75
	6.1 I – Development by Exile		77
		6.1.1 Constructing Development Between Non-state Actors	78
		6.1.2 Migration Leads to Development	80
		6.1.3 Development Leads to Migration	81
		6.1.4 Highly Differentiated Situations Across the World	82
		6.1.5 The Win-Win-Win Approach	84
	6.2 Conclusion		84
	References		84
Conclusion of the Book			87
Bibliography			91

About the Author

Catherine Wihtol de Wenden is a political scientist (Sciences Po Paris) and is graduated in public law (University Paris I Panthéon Sorbonne). Her research has been focused on the political approach to immigration in France and Europe, and subsequently at the global level, with the use of field studies and comparative work. She is Senior Research Fellow Emerita at CNRS and teaches at Sciences Po Paris. She was President of the Research Committee "Migration" of the International Sociological Association (ISA) from 2002 to 2008, and she is a member of the Scientific Committee of the Museum of Immigration in Paris. Her most recent book publications are *La question migratoire au XXIème siècle: Migrants, réfugiés et relations internationales* (Presses de Sciences Po, 2017, 3rd edition), *Faut-il ouvrir les frontières?* (Presses de Sciences Po, 2017, 3rd edition), *Géopolitique des migrations* (Eyrolles, 2019), *Immigration: Chance ou menace?* (First, 2020), *Atlas des migrations* (Autrement, 2021, 6th edition), and *Figures de l'Autre: Perceptions de l'immigration en France 1870-2022* (CNRS Editions, 2022).

Chapter 1
International Migration as a World Issue

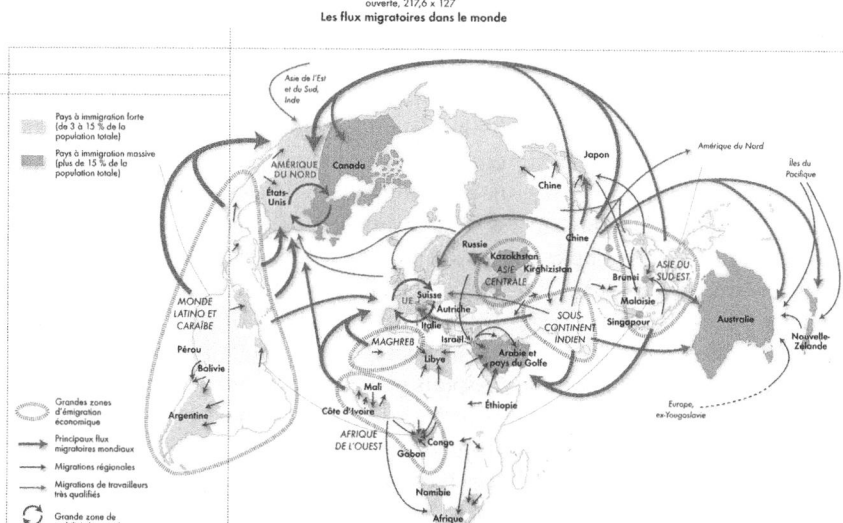

Migration flows in the world
Europe: EU (no need to translate the other names Italy, Switzerland)
Africa: Western Africa (Mali, Ivory Coast), Maghreb (Libya), South Africa
Middle East: Israel, Gulf States
Russia, Central Asia, Kazakhstan
Asia: India, China, Japan
South-East Asia: Malaysia, Singapore
Australia, New Zealand
North America: USA, Canada
Latin America and Caribbean's: Peru, Bolivia, Argentina
Source: OECD, SOPEMI (2020)

In the twenty-first century, migration has become a global phenomenon, not only because of the sheer number of people involved in migratory flows throughout the world (284 million international migrants, or 3% of the world population), but above all because of its ubiquity: no region, no country in the world is unaffected by migratory flows, and all countries in the world are involved either in emigration, or in immigration, or as a transit country. Most countries are involved in all three of these processes to some extent.

1.1 The Globalisation of Migration

This trend towards the globalisation of migration has been increasing sharply since the 1990s, when the fall of the Iron Curtain suddenly granted a right to exit one's country to many inhabitants of the former Soviet Union and Eastern Bloc. Around the same time, many countries in the Global South started to grant passports more readily to their citizens. These countries had formerly been reluctant to give out substantial numbers of passports to their nationals, sometimes because they considered that their population was their main resource, and sometimes because they feared that their nationals abroad might endanger internal political stability.

Both these factors contributed to the development of a much more extensive right to emigration. At the same time, this growing right to leave ran up against a growing difficulty of entry into countries of immigration, who increased their visa requirements. Now, according to a report by the International Association of Air Transportation (IATA) in 2021, the right to mobility is closely linked to access to national passports that grant access to large numbers of countries without a requirement for visas. For example, Japanese and Singaporean passports grant access to 192 countries without visas, for South Korean passports the figure is 190, for EU Member States the figure varies between 186 and 189, for the US it is 186, and Australian and Canadian passports grant access to 185 countries. The last place is occupied by Afghanistan, whose passports grant access to only 26 countries without a visa, mostly neighbouring and poor countries. This context plays a determining role in the possibilities of mobility open to people throughout the world, and also helps to explain the increasing role played by human smuggling and trafficking.

1.2 Other Important Developments Over the Last 30 Years

Recent decades have seen a diversification of migration flows: these now include 110 million refugees and asylum seekers (including 27.1 million statutory refugees as recognised under the Geneva Convention of 1951), 6 million Palestinians recognised as displaced persons by the United Nations Relief and Works Agency for Palestine Refugees (UNWRA), and various other forms of humanitarian and temporary statuses that have been granted in response to forced migration.

These increasingly diverse migration flows now include large numbers of women (half of global migration flows), children (with a particular increase in numbers of unaccompanied minors), highly skilled migrants, families (especially in longstanding immigration countries such as the US and some European countries), workers (particularly from the Global South), and many people without any precise status: irregular migrants or so-called "illegals" (approximately 11 million in the US and 5 million in Europe), environmentally displaced persons (approximately 50 million), and stateless people without any citizenship, such as in Myanmar and Bangladesh, but also in many other places (4 million, UNHCR report 2023) of statelessness people.

1.2 Other Important Developments Over the Last 30 Years

Another major development is that the scale of migration flows to the Global South (140 million) has reached the scale of migration flows to the Global North (140 million), if we include in these figures North-North and South-South migration as well as migration between these two areas. It is a very new phenomenon for the combined number of South-North migrants (particularly families, workers, refugees, and students) and North-North migrants (skilled people, students with exchange programmes, tourists) to be matched by the combined number of North-South migrants (skilled workers driven from the North to the South by the economic crisis, older people looking for better weather, entrepreneurship by second and third generation migrants moving to the countries of their parents or grandparents, people seeking to exploit raw materials) and South-South migrants (those moving to countries with emerging economies and Gulf states, refugees, and also environmentally displaced persons).

There is an increasing tendency for the categories of migrants to be blurred, as many people involved in family reunifications or seeking asylum are also looking for jobs. The sociological profiles associated with these different categories has become much closer, whereas it was previously far easier to distinguish, for example, between dissidents from the Soviet Union and illiterate workers travelling to make up labour shortages in Western Europe. Now, statistically, a migrant entering a country will have a level of qualification higher than the average of the population of that country, and will be three times more productive than in their country of origin. Depending on their level of qualification, they may adopt one of the many possible statuses open to them. The closure of European borders to low-skilled labour migration from the 1970s onwards, and the increasing focus on border control as the main instrument of restrictive migration policies (including asylum policies), has led to a more complex mix of migration flows. In many cases, claiming asylum offers the only means of attaining a right to remain in the country of destination without passports and visas.

All these developments over the last 30 years have brought two broad trends into stark contrast: on the one hand, an aspiration towards a human right to mobility in an era of modernity, and on the other hand, the growth of restrictive policies aimed at curtailing that right. Certain social changes across the world are contributing to these trends. Urbanisation is increasing across the planet, especially in Africa, which is projected to change from a 70% rural population in 1950 to a 70% urban population by 2050. Demography is another crucial issue, since there is a large contrast between the ageing populations of the Global North (where the median age is 40 years old) and younger populations of the Global South (with a median age, for example, of 25 in the Maghreb and 19 in Sub-Saharan Africa). The large numbers of older people reaching the so-called "fourth age" is creating a growing demand for new jobs in care, largely provided by migration. Meanwhile, jobs in agriculture or in services that are traditionally associated with migrant workers continue to be dependent on migration, and some highly qualified jobs are proving difficult to fill, such as medical workers in rural areas of the Global North. In the last 30 years, most countries in the Global North have developed more security-orientated immigration policies, with the aim of closing borders to newcomers, even though this generally contradicts the need for migration in order to make up for labour shortages and maintain competitiveness and creativity. There is therefore a conflict between the imperatives of economic liberalism at the global level and nationalist and security concerns that dominate politics at the level of individual states. In most cases, the latter have the upper hand in determining policy, owing to the pressure of public opinion. The consequence of this is an emphasis on security instead of providing hospitality to migrants (including refugees).

This securitisation of borders has forced migrants to make a choice, in the words of Aristide Zolberg (1978), between "the main gate and the back door". As Zolberg explains, "the illegals are victims of the hypocrisy of political decision-makers who admit this situation". The main immigration countries are leading this trend towards the restriction of immigration policies. Since every state defines its own conditions for entry, these decisions at the national level shape and limit the right to mobility at the global level. The right to exit, which became a universal right protected by a number of international conventions (the UN Declaration of 1948, the Geneva Convention on Refugees of 1951, the UN Convention of 1990 on the rights of migrant workers) now runs up against the difficulty of entry, which depends on decisions made by nation states.

The consequence of this disequilibrium is to give a very important role to the management of borders. For migrants travelling from countries in the Global North to those in the Global South, exit and entry are both easy, but the rights of migrants may be restricted in the countries of destination (access to citizenship or property ownership, for example). For migration between countries within the Global North (North-North migration) people similarly enjoy easy exit and entry (without visas in many cases), and also have rights in the countries of destination that are close to those of citizens. However, in the case of South-North migration, it is now easy to leave but difficult to enter, to the extent that these journeys result in large numbers of deaths at or near borders (for example, in the Mediterranean and at the US/Mexico border). Nonetheless, a legal migrant, after spending some years of residence in their country of destination, may come to enjoy similar rights to those of citizens, or even gain access to citizenship. In the case of South-South migration, no rights are recognised in most cases, but entry and residence are tolerated for asylum seekers, and some countries link residence with work (notably the Gulf states).

Another consequence of this disequilibrium is the disproportionate role played by major immigration states in shaping migration regimes: the US, Canada, certain European states, Japan, and Australia all play a major role in defining the main rules of the migration regime, while none of these have ratified the UN International Convention on the Protection of the Rights of All Migrant Workers and Members of Their Families (ICRMW). This convention of 1990 was intended to be signed by all UN Member States, but has so far been ratified by only 56 states, all from the Global South. States in the Global North have been reluctant to ratify it owing to the rights that it confers on irregular migrants (so-called "illegals") and asylum seekers. Global migration governance has therefore been shaped to a large extent by the strongest countries, often against the wishes of small states and those in the Global South, and in ways that produce many unfortunate results: large numbers of irregular migrants, unaccompanied minors, and asylum seekers without recognition of refugee status, the extensive use of camps, prisons, and repatriations, and even large numbers of deaths.

1.2.1 *I – The Main Factors Affecting Migration*

Migration is a structural phenomenon, rooted in migration systems. The concept of migration systems was first developed by Douglas Massey (2003), who defined it in relation to the US/Mexico region. Most migration systems arise in response to an accumulation of different types of disparities or gaps: in demographics, economics, culture, and politics (notably the difference between democratic and authoritarian regimes). Where a solution to these "gaps" does not present itself within regions of departure, candidates for migration perceive a possible solution in the option of "exiting" that country or region. In this world of restrictive border policies (two-thirds of the population of the planet do not have the right to move freely outside the borders of their country), many new actors are confronting this international order dominated by the power of individual nation states (Sassen, 1996). Transnational networks are creating many linkages across borders, including family networks, networks facilitated by new technologies (TV, mobile phones, the internet), and networks of remittances sent by migrants to their families, which amounted to $550 billion in 2021, that is, more than all the public funds devoted to development policies. The development of family networks is supported by second or third generation migrants gaining access to dual citizenship, thus allowing them to move across borders more easily. The general aspiration of these actors is for easier access to mobility, including exit, entry, and return. Indeed, this easier mobility was previously possible in many earlier contexts, particularly during the period of large-scale labour migration, which came to an end in Europe in the mid-1970s and at the US/Mexico border in 1965 (the end of the "Bracero Program"). Conversely, mobility became possible from East to West in Europe after the fall of the Berlin Wall and of the Iron Curtain in 1989, leading to the adoption of mobility as a way of life.

In the mid-1980s and early 1990s, new paradigms of migration transformed former emigration countries into countries of immigration and transit. For example, Italy, Spain, Portugal, Greece, and Malta became immigration countries, partly owing to the closure of borders within Europe. Borders were also effectively externalised beyond Europe itself, since Morocco, Tunisia, Algeria, Libya, Turkey, and certain Sub-Saharan African countries were forced by Europe to accept policies of repatriation and to control departures from their own borders. In populations on the southern rim of the Mediterranean, there was a growing demand for visas to allow young people – often well-educated but with limited prospects for work – to find new opportunities. Some regions that have been involved in emigration for a long time (such as the valley of the Senegal river, the north of Morocco, and Berber regions in Algeria) have a strong dependency on migration. This is now also the case for Poland, Romania, and Bulgaria thanks to the new possibilities for mobility between countries of the European Union. The externalisation of borders into the southern Mediterranean region is also having the effect of transforming these countries into countries of transit: people on the move in these contexts are referred to as "transmigrants", reflecting their provisional situation. The same phenomenon can now also be observed in the US, Mexico, and Central America: migrants from Central America are first moving to Mexico, where some of them stay because entry into the US is made more difficult by the existence of drug cartels. Just as migrants from Sub-Saharan countries sometimes end up remaining in Morocco, migrants from Central America may end up in a long-term state of "transit" in Mexico. The externalisation of borders is thus extending to greater distances, giving rise to new migration routes, and creating new sites of transmigration, such as Niger or Mauritania.

One of the greatest drivers of migration flows is the sense of hopelessness and insecurity experienced by those exposed to situations of war. Most migrants are young, urbanised, educated, and informed, yet consider that there is no future or suitable employment for them in their countries of origin. They sometimes say that they are already dead before they face possible death in the Mediterranean sea or at the Mexican border. More than half of young people in the Global South want to leave their countries of origin. Those who end up leaving are not the poorest, but rather those who have the means to develop a project, access to international networks, and the possibility of raising money to pay people smugglers if they cannot get a visa.

1.2.2 II – The Various Forms of Mobility

The available statistics related to migration mostly describe regular or legal migration. These include data from the SOPEMI reports of the Organisation for Economic Co-operation and Development (OECD), the annual reports produced by the United Nations Department of Economic and Social Affairs (UNDESA), and the United Nations High Commissioner for Refugees (UNHCR), which issues annual data on refugees and asylum seekers at the global level. Most legal migrants belong to three categories: workers, family reunification, and refugees. There has also been a significant rise in the numbers of international students, short-term (seasonal) migration, and rich people from poor countries who are able to gain access to residence permits owing to their investments, funds, trading activity, or real estate assets. Some new migration flows are emerging but in small numbers: migration for access to health services, to flee sexual mistreatment (harassment, discrimination on grounds of sexual orientation, etc.), and to escape from environmental threats. Across the world, the scale of migration flows has grown form 77 million people in 1975, to 120 million by the end of the 1990s, and now to 284 million. In other words, it has increased by a factor of 3.5 over 45 years. However, migration flows and patterns of settlement have also developed within certain regions. We can thus observe a distinct Euro-Mediterranean Space and a distinct US-Mexican Space, which make up two of the most substantial migration flows in the world: most migrants entering Europe depart from countries on the southern rim of the Mediterranean, while Mexicans and Central Americans make up half of all migrants entering the US. South America is in itself a migration region, with new migration flows arising from Colombia, Bolivia, Ecuador, Peru, and Venezuela, heading towards Brazil, Argentina, Uruguay, and Chile. After European countries and the US, the next largest destination (in terms of numbers of migrants) is made up of the Gulf states, which receive large numbers of South-South migrants, primarily from Arab countries, but also from emigration countries as far away as Pakistan, the Philippines, and some Sub-Saharan countries. The fourth largest destination is Russia, which primarily receives migrants from states that formerly belonged to the Soviet Union (particularly in the South Caucasus and Central Asia), owing to the strength of their former links (language, knowledge of Russian administration, and the existence of short-term visas for work). Turkey is also a major country of immigration and transit, owing to the recent refugee crisis (producing migration flows from Iraq, Iran, and Syria), while also remaining the largest country of emigration to Europe (there are 4.4 million Turks in Europe, mainly in Germany). Japan, South Africa, and Australia also receive migration flows from the region immediately around them. For all these immigration countries, the number of migrants entering from countries in the same region is greater than the number of migrants entering from other regions. This fact illustrates the general tendency towards the regionalisation of migration flows. This trend can be observed in the development of a number of new regional spaces across the world, such as migration within Europe (with the opening of borders between European countries and the closure of borders to non-Europeans), the Nordic Space (including some countries that are not EU Member States), the Economic Community of West African States (ECOWAS) (in spite of conflicts in the region), the Trans-Tasman Travel Agreement (TTTA) between Australia and New Zealand, the Association of Southeast Asian Nations (ASEAN), which helps South Asian emigration countries to engage with other Asian countries, the Union of South American Nations (UNASUR), and the Southern African Development Community (SADC), which strengthens ties between South Africa and its neighbours. Turkey has also opened its borders to more than 40 countries in order to facilitate trade and tourism, and to attract workers from Russia. There are also a number of regional spaces where free circulation is possible in principle, but where mobility is complicated by the existence of conflict zones.

Along with these various kinds of mobility, we can observe new patterns and statuses of migration: commuters across borders (such as between countries of Eastern and Western Europe, since the fall of the Iron Curtain), seasonal workers who sometimes remain illegally in the immigration country waiting for new seasonal work, irregular migrants who remain in place until they attain a regularisation of their status, formal or informal family reunifications, unaccompanied minors sometimes spending years on the road, deciding whether to continue, return, or stay where they are (sometimes called "transmigrants"), and various forms of citizenship, statelessness, and dual nationality (particularly for second generation migrants).

We are therefore witnessing, at the same time, the opening of many borders and the closure or strengthening of many others. Over 50,000 deaths have been counted in the Mediterranean Sea since the end of 1990s. European policies have always responded to the perceived "migration crisis" with an increasing securitisation of borders, leading to greater expense for border controls, and more deaths.

1.3 The Impact of the COVID-19 Pandemic: Reinforcing the Migration Gap Between North and South

This situation in which almost no migration took place over the course of several months led to a fall in remittances of 20%, according to the World Bank (the total figure was $530 billion in 2019). This phenomenon could be observed both in the European/Mediterranean region, and across North, Central, and South America. In India, the COVID-19 pandemic had a drastic effect on internal migration: hundreds of thousands of people travelled from the north to the south of the country at the beginning of the crisis, exacerbating the spread of disease, which led to large numbers of deaths, and consequently large numbers of children becoming orphans, with limited prospects for their future education. In Venezuela, many de facto refugees returned home from Colombia or Brazil, where they had sought shelter. In Africa, which was struck by COVID-19 later in 2020, the closing of borders all around the planet created particular challenges, since most employment there is informal and social welfare is largely absent. The African continent also closed its borders, which had the effect of increasing inequalities (Green, 2020). Countries in the south of Africa still have a poor level of vaccination coverage, but nonetheless have a relatively low rate of deaths. Whereas Europeans and Americans had not experienced such a large-scale pandemic for many years, African populations had already been living with pandemics: notably malaria (400,000 deaths per year in Sub-Saharan Africa), tuberculosis, and HIV (350,000 deaths).

When migration largely came to a halt in 2020, the phenomenon had an impact on immigration countries, creating shortages in some sectors of the labour market (agriculture, healthcare, and construction, as well as a reduction in the number of foreign students in higher education). This also had the effect of increasing competition between these rich immigration countries to recruit highly qualified people and carers for the older population. Meanwhile, migrants who had already settled in these countries saw a deterioration in their situation, due to unemployment, the difficulty of accessing public services and healthcare, and the higher mortality of ethnic minorities compared with other populations. In emigration countries in the Global South, the decline in remittances from diasporic migration drastically reduced the resources available to Sub-Saharan countries. The general decrease in employment, the increasing precarity of migrants, and the reduction in economic activity paired with labour shortages in certain sectors all brought to light the strong, interconnected dependency on migration of both Western (immigration) countries and Southern (emigration) countries. However, despite the stark demonstration of this interdependency, immigration countries did not decide to change their migration policies after the COVID-19 crisis in response to labour shortages.

Along with the general globalisation of migration flows, migration is therefore also structured across the world in a series of regionalised systems, determined by complex systems of complementarities and relationships of demographic and economic supply and demand. In the Global South, development is not, in the short term, an alternative to migration. In the past, Southern European countries ceased to be countries of emigration when they experienced economic growth and became more democratic. The same is also true for Eastern Europe, whose circular migration is due to their entry into the EU. In countries on the southern rim of the Mediterranean, we can expect that development (both economic and political) and demographic transition will weaken the strongest pressures driving the emigration of low-skilled workers.

The 2009 Report of the United Nations Development Programme (UNDP) declared that mobility had become a major factor in human development. Overall, migration improves standards of living, reduces risks (economic, political, social, and health-related), particularly in unsafe countries of origin without systems of health or social insurance, and it provides resources from remittances to families remaining in emigration countries. Mobility supports the development of transnational economic networks, decreases unemployment, exports social dissent, and allows those who remain in place to live better.

1.3.1 III – Migration in the Euro-Mediterranean Space: A Case Study

Of the 22 countries bordering the Mediterranean Sea, most have been emigration countries in the past (such as Southern European countries), or remain so (such as Egypt). Many of them, including Turkey and countries of the Maghreb, have become countries of emigration, immigration, and also transit, since they receive migrants travelling from the south who are ultimately trying to reach Europe. The Euro-Mediterranean Space is consequently the location of some of the largest migration flows in the world.

The Euro-Mediterranean Space features some of the sharpest contrasts in the world between the countries on its northern and southern rim – demographically, economically, socially, politically, and culturally – in spite of their geographical proximity and the many structures of dialogue and transnational networks that exist. This explains why it is one of the most intense sites of migration flows in the world. Together with the rest of Europe, it makes up a regional "migration system", a space of exchanges, where the demand for labour force meets a supply of migrant workers, and where most migration flows remain within the sphere of the region, reinforced by existing legal and irregular networks (families, transnational economies, and refugee flows). However, migration is often perceived as a problem in the Euro-Mediterranean political agenda, where it is mostly addressed through the increased securitisation of borders and the fight against people smuggling and trafficking. Meanwhile, widening imbalances in demographics and labour demands suggest that it could experience even great mobility in the future.

Aside from the Balkan region, five major European countries have a Mediterranean coast: France and the so called "PIGS" (Portugal, Italy, Greece, and Spain). These are joined by two smaller countries: Cyprus and Malta. All of them play a major role in receiving immigration from the southern coast of the Mediterranean, forming "migratory pairs" (where migrants from one country travel to one main immigration country, such as Algerians travelling to France, which receives 92% of Algerian migrants to Europe) or "quasi diasporas". In the latter case, migrants from one country are found in significant numbers in several European countries, connected by many transnational linkages, which are sometimes made by migrants and sometimes encouraged by their emigration countries. This is true of Turkish and Moroccan migrants, who constitute the two biggest extra-European groups in Europe. In spite of these similarities, all European countries with Mediterranean coasts have several specificities. France is strongly marked by its colonial past and its long immigration history, which explains why Algerians are the second largest immigrant group (after Portuguese, and followed by Moroccans). Immigrants to Italy are made up several main nationalities, including Albanians, Romanians, and Moroccans. In Spain, Moroccans make up the largest immigrant group. Portugal receives significant numbers of immigrants from Spain and Romania. In Greece, which before 2004 had no land border with an EU Member State, the largest immigrant group is Albanian, followed by immigrants from other neighbours (Bulgarians, Romanians), and large numbers of asylum seekers from Syria. The importance of tourism, construction, services, and agriculture in Spain and Italy explains the significant rise in immigration to these countries, which in recent years have become the second and third countries of immigration in Europe, overtaking France and the United Kingdom. The 2008 economic crisis had a major impact on the Spanish economy, which had been built on the economic boom of the 2000s, and since this time immigrants have increasingly been seen as competing with nationals on the labour market (just as Polish immigrants were perceived in this way in the UK before the latter left the EU at the end of 2020).

Since the mid-1990s, Southern European countries have attempted to develop a migration regime including states from the southern Mediterranean coast, in the context of the Euro-Mediterranean Space: the Barcelona Agreements of 1995–2005 were concerned, among things, with migration, and although they were considered to be only a partial success, they aimed to improve visa systems for mobility and trade, despite the reinforcement of the fight against irregular transit and terrorism. However, they were more orientated towards opening borders to trade than towards facilitating human mobility, much like the NAFTA agreements between Mexico, the US, and Canada. Discussion of migration at European summits is mostly directed towards the fight against illegal migration, with the consequence of turning the Mediterranean Sea into one of the largest cemeteries in the world for irregular migrants. Some locations, such as the Canary Islands, Malta, Lampedusa, and certain Greek islands have received significant flows of irregular migration, despite the efforts of Frontex, the European police force for border control. European efforts have also been directed towards the externalisation of borders, most recently focusing on Libya and Turkey as partners in bilateral agreements or multilateral ones involving several European countries.

Countries on the southern Mediterranean coast, rather than presenting a united front towards Europe, have tended to engage in competition with one another to make bilateral agreements with European countries. This situation has been exacerbated by several conflicts, such as that between Algeria and Morocco, the complex situation in Israel/Palestine, and also in Cyprus. The entry of the new Eastern European states into the EU was perceived as another element of competition by countries on the southern Mediterranean coast, since, from 2004, these new entrants to the EU gradually came to benefit from freedom of movement, work, and settlement. These Eastern European migrants were generally better educated than those from the southern Mediterranean coast, and were less frequently victims of discrimination (with the notable exception of Roma populations). They therefore found it easier to enter Western European labour markets, and those of some Southern European countries, such as Spain, Italy, and Portugal. These Eastern European countries also made bilateral agreements with countries of Western and Southern Europe regarding work in agriculture, construction, services, and tourism. The freedoms accorded to Eastern European countries have been viewed dimly by countries of the Maghreb, in light of the circulation agreements that the latter had formerly concluded with European countries after decolonisation (such as the Evian agreements providing for free circulation between Algeria and France between 1962 and 1973), and the existence of close links due to transnational family networks.

The rapid changes in demographics across the Euro-Mediterranean Space constitute one of the most important factors affecting the migration regime. Southern European countries that had been exporters of labour from the 1950s to the 1970s, such as Italy and Spain, are now experiencing slowing population growth, to the extent that their population is projected to be less in 2030 than it is at present. This change explains the increasing need in these countries for labour force, which is also required to support their tourism industries and the long-term settlement of older people from Northern European countries (Germans and British in Spain, British in southern Portugal and France, and various nationalities in Italy and Greece, while Bulgaria is trying to attract lower-paid and elderly Europeans). These same Southern European countries also have growing numbers of older people among their own nationals, which creates an additional need for care: care workers and nurses are moving to Italy, Spain, and Portugal from Poland, Ukraine, and Romania, thereby creating a "care drain" in Balkan countries such as Romania and Bulgaria.

Meanwhile, the countries of the Maghreb have also entered a period of demographic transition, experiencing both a decrease in births due to family planning, and a decrease in deaths due to improvements in health care. The consequences of this are mixed: at present, more people have the means to travel abroad, as they have fewer children and there are still enough younger and middle-aged people to look after the elderly, whereas in the future the ratio of younger people to older people will make it more difficult to travel abroad because of the shortage of people to care for the elderly. These countries are experiencing transit migration, which sometimes becomes a migration of settlement (migrants to these countries from the south typically practise trades and casual work), and they are being urged by Europe to become gatekeepers of European borders through repatriation agreements. This externalisation of European borders to countries of the southern Mediterranean coast is carried out through the use of targets in the context of the European Pacts on Immigration and Asylum (2008, 2014, 2020), and negotiated in exchange for development policies or visas for the elites.

Turkey, in addition to experiencing the same demographic transition as the countries of the Maghreb, has become a haven for refugees coming from Syria, Iraq, and Afghanistan. Following the refugee crisis of 2015 and the EU-Turkey agreement of 2016, it has consequently become a country at the intersection of massive migration flows.

It is therefore clear that the immigration landscape in the Euro-Mediterranean Space will be very different in 20 years from what it is now. Immigration flows from Sub-Saharan Africa and possibly from the Middle East are expected to continue, but with a decrease in migration from the immediate southern rim. However, environmental and climatic changes may accelerate migration from regions threatened by desertification (such as the south of Morocco, which is vulnerable to the expansion of the Sahara Desert), and environmentally displaced persons without any means of regular migration may seek refugee status. The ongoing political conflicts are also likely to continue to play a role.

Many transnational networks spanning the two sides of the Mediterranean Sea have developed with the support of associations. Emigration countries such as Morocco and Turkey have been very active in integrating their diasporas abroad in their diplomatic efforts. They have therefore supported those diasporas in forming national associations, sending remittances, seeking dual citizenship, and using elites to build bridges with countries of departure. The strength of their bargaining position is manifested in bilateral and multilateral agreements in which commitments towards the repatriation of irregular migrants is exchanged for trade agreements and development policies involving non-state actors, as well as favourable migration regimes for elites. Strong similarities can be found between this situation and that which exists between Mexico and the US.

Many Northern European countries have little interest in the Mediterranean region, being more focused on their immediate neighbourhoods. These countries prefer to support the reinforcement of borders in Southern Europe and on the southern rim of the Mediterranean, using tools of border control such as the Schengen Information System (SIS), Eurodac (a digital system for the control of asylum seekers), Spain's Sistema Integrado de Vigilancia del Exterior (SIVE), and especially Frontex, whose budget grew from €5 million in 2005 to €543 million in 2020. More broadly, Northern European countries lend legitimacy to the approach to migration control that consists in linking it with the fight against terrorism.

Europe has struggled to adapt to its situation as a land of immigration, since it was formerly a place of departure. European identity, as well as individual national identities, are not accustomed to the idea that immigration can contribute to the building of EU Nation States. The rise in far right populism in many European countries shows that there remains a significant reluctance to recognise even the legitimacy of migration, let alone its potential benefits. Europe is an immigration space in spite of itself, much like Japan, the Gulf States, and all those regions that find themselves heavily dependent on migration for demographic and economic reasons.

1.4 Conclusion

The COVID-19 crisis has highlighted the dependency of immigration countries on foreign labour, both from within Europe and from outside Europe. The decline in economic activity first led to a loss of employment for most foreign workers. In this climate of labour shortages, Italy and Portugal legalised their irregular workers employed in the care sector. In Germany, seasonal agriculture faced particular challenges from the scarcity of foreign workers, especially those from Ukraine. In the UK, many Polish workers left in the wake of the Brexit vote, in response to a perceived hostility towards workers from Europe, and many Romanian agricultural workers left in 2020 the context of the COVID-19 crisis. Austria, despite a context of public opinion that was hostile to migration, reopened its borders to care workers for older people. Meanwhile, Ukrainians left Poland, owing to a shortage of jobs, returning to their homes in Ukraine. In Spain, the shortage of Moroccan women workers collecting strawberries in spring caused particular problems, as Spanish workers are rarely willing to do this work. In the south of France, a lack of flexibility in the labour market meant that the departure of Moroccan migrant agricultural workers could not be compensated for by employing French people.

References

Green, T. (2020). *The Covid consensus: The new politics of global inequalities.* Hurst.
Massey, D. (2003). A synthetic theory of international migration. In *World in the mirror of international migration* (pp. 138–161). Max Press.
OECD, SOPEMI. (2020). *Perspectives on international migrations* (Annual report 2020).
Sassen, S. (1996). *Losing control? Sovereignty in an age of globalisation.* Columbia University Press.
Zolberg, A. (1978). International policies in a changing world system. In W. McNeill & R. Adams (Eds.), *Human migrations: Patterns and policies* (pp. 5–27). Indiana University Press.

Open Access This chapter is licensed under the terms of the Creative Commons Attribution 4.0 International License (http://creativecommons.org/licenses/by/4.0/), which permits use, sharing, adaptation, distribution and reproduction in any medium or format, as long as you give appropriate credit to the original author(s) and the source, provide a link to the Creative Commons license and indicate if changes were made.

The images or other third party material in this chapter are included in the chapter's Creative Commons license, unless indicated otherwise in a credit line to the material. If material is not included in the chapter's Creative Commons license and your intended use is not permitted by statutory regulation or exceeds the permitted use, you will need to obtain permission directly from the copyright holder.

Chapter 2
Immigration Policies

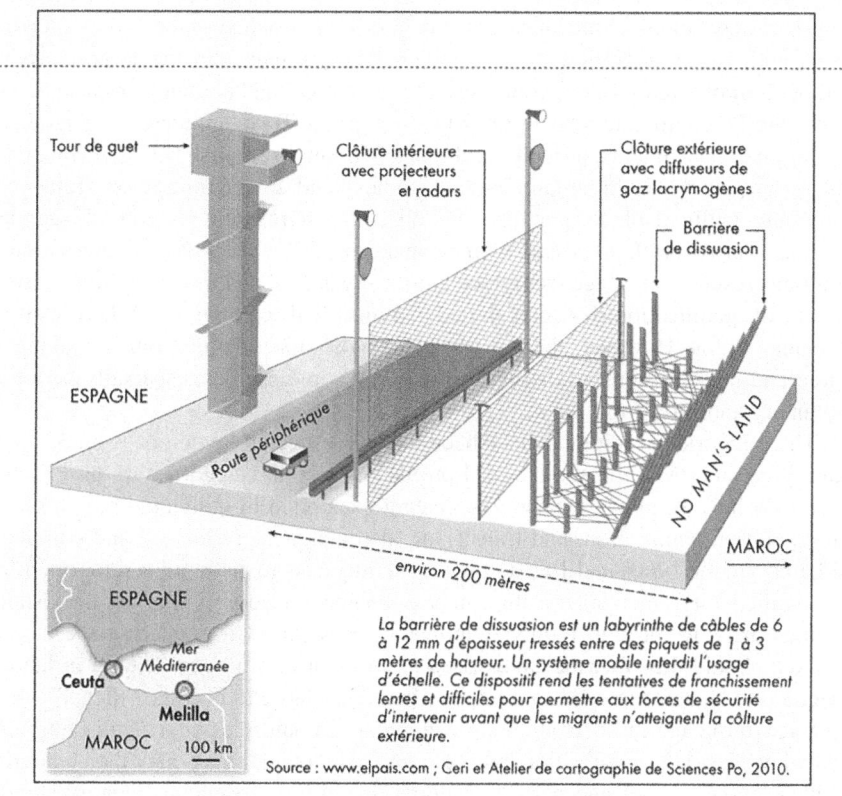

The Melilla-Ceuta border
Spain Morocco, Internal fence, external fence, no man's land, roughly 200 meters

2.1 Who Is an International Migrant?

An international migrant is defined as somebody who lives in a different country from that in which they were born, irrespective of their nationality. According to this definition, there are 284 million international migrants in the world (UNDESA Report, 2021), a number which has rapidly grown since the 1990s (120 million). However, there is a far greater number of internal migrants, travelling within national borders, currently standing at 740 million. Whereas "migrants" are defined geographically (mobility across borders for more than 1 year), the "foreigner" is defined legally, as a non-national. There are therefore always more international migrants than there are foreigners, since some migrants are non-nationals in their place of residence, while others have naturalised to become nationals. Irregular migrants are not included in international and internal statistics. International migrants may belong to one of several categories, in a context of blurred categorisations and mixed migration flows. Foreign workers make up the largest group, although in old immigration countries, such as the US and certain European countries, family reunification makes up the largest group. There are increasing numbers of international students, as well as refugees. We can distinguish between voluntary migration (work, family reunification, studies) and forced migration (refugees, environmentally displaced persons), and observe patterns with regard to the gender of migrants (overall, men and women make up 52% and 48% of international migrants respectively), age (senior, economically active, and minor migrants), their degree of qualification (broadly, skilled and unskilled migrants), and their legal or irregular status. However, the increasing globalisation of migration is making it more and more difficult to distinguish between some profiles, especially between voluntary and forced migrants.

The categories of migrants have been blurred (especially workers, refugees, and family members) as the sociological profiles of several categories are now closer than they have been in the past. The categories applied to individual nation states (immigration, emigration, and transit) are also increasingly blurred and complex. Whereas, in the 1960s and 1970s, it was generally easy to distinguish refugees from unqualified migrant workers, they now often have a very similar profile. Many women arriving through family reunification procedures are entering the labour market: should they then be categorised in terms of family reunification or labour migration? Unaccompanied minors are often considered to become "illegal" when they reach the age of 18. Somebody who enters a country as an irregular migrant, but whose level of qualification helps them to gain a legal status may then enter the skilled labour market and perhaps acquire citizenship. To which category should they be assigned? We could point to many other such examples of blurred categories, in this context of increasing divergences between legal categories and sociological or economic realities.

2.1.1 I – Literature Review

Previously, most research on migration was conducted either at the micro-level or with a focus on a specific immigration country. However, more lately a large number of authors have analysed migration at a global level and as an international relations issue. Among these authors, we have chosen a small number whose approach is particularly illustrative of developments in the field.

2.2 Stephen Castles: International Migration as a Global Issue

Stephen Castles was one of the first sociologists of migration to develop an approach to migration at the global level. In so doing, he placed a particular emphasis on Asia and Oceania as new migration regions. His innovative approach to migration studies consists in both multi-disciplinary analysis (with a principle grounding in sociology) and a comparative perspective, in which different regional migration spaces and systems are viewed within a global context. After a long stay in Europe (Frankfurt, the EU Institute in Florence, and Oxford) and Wollongong, Australia, he concluded his academic career at the University of Sydney.

The global perspective on migration that Stephen Castles developed at the end of the twentieth century is now very well-known from his book *The Age of Migration*, written initially with Mark Miller, formerly chief editor of *International Migration Review* in New York, and with Hein De Haas from the fifth edition of 2014, a researcher at the University of Oxford and now a professor in the Netherlands (Castles et al., 2014). The book covers the whole world, with a chapter on migration theories and a regional analysis of migration systems. The originality of this book written for students lies in its excellent contributions on Europe, the US, and Asia. It develops a focus on the regionalisation of migration flows in regional migration systems, and also presents an analysis of migration and integration policies at the global scale.

Stephen Castles also links the analysis of migration spaces and policies with the question of citizenship. On the subject of citizenship and multiculturalism, he stresses the concept of negotiating citizenship. His main contribution on this issue (Castles & Davidson, 2000) is a large-scale reflection on citizenship as belonging and its connection to migration issues, starting from the Australian case, but then extending to a comparative approach with European countries. He demonstrated the extent to which the content of multicultural citizenship is a matter for negotiation in countries of migration of settlement. In the case of Australia, an initial dream of a "white Australia" made up of populations of British background was eventually replaced owing to the rise of migration from other areas and a focus on Aboriginals' rights, which brought about a change in the national definition of "who belongs". Castles and Davidson thus show how multiculturalism was inserted into the

Australian Constitution, and how this pragmatic adaptation was gradually transformed into a theoretical model. This process invites comparisons with Canada, which was the first country to formally define a system of multiculturalism, initially as a bi-national state, and later as a country of migration of settlement, taking into account (as in Australia) the existence of autochthonous natives.

2.3 James Hollifield: The Contemporary Contradictions of Economic Liberalism and Security-Based Politics, from a Comparative Perspective

James Hollifield is Professor of Political Science at Southern Methodist University (SMU), in Texas. He is a Global Fellow and Public Policy Scholar at the Wilson Center, and Ora Nixon Arnold Professor of International Political Economy and Director of the John G. Tower Center for Public Policy and International Affairs at SMU. He is a well-known specialist of France and other European countries, and a comparatist of migration policies implemented by European countries and the US. He has published several books, including a collection on *Migration Theory* with Karolyn Brettell (2014). In his book *Immigrants, Markets and States: American Policy and Politics* (1992), and in later comparative research on Europe, Hollifield defines what he calls "the liberal paradox" presented by the contradictions between, on the one hand, immigration policies inspired by free markets and economic liberalism in the biggest immigration countries of the Global North, and on the other hand, the growing securitisation and closure of borders in those same countries. He analyses the conflicts of interest between employers and policy decision makers in the American case, but also in most European countries (notably France, Germany, the UK, and Italy), as well as in Japan. But the findings of this analysis are now being challenged by the changing nature of migration.

In the French case, for example, traditional actors such as employers and trade unions played a major role in decision-making processes between 1945 and 1975, but they lost influence between 1980 and 2020, when deindustrialisation and unemployment became prominent factors. Since 1975, decision-makers have been influenced far less by employers than by their fear of the public opinion of voters on the political far right. As the vast majority of legal newcomers are not workers, but asylum seekers, students, and migrants involved in family reunifications, the relevance of the "liberal paradox" (which involves the perspective of employers) is necessarily reduced.

Public opinion is now the most important factor in the decision-making process. For quite a long period (1945–1975), immigration was a depoliticised issue (Wihtol de Wenden, 1988). This was due to the need for immigrant workers to support the booming economy. The rise of the far right in the 1980s, which placed immigration at the core of its political programme, played a major role in making it a prominent political question. In many cases, questions of security now dominate discussions of migration, and symbolic rather than pragmatic policies are used to reassure the right-wing vote.

The role of civil society (NGOs, human rights associations, social solidarity associations, and churches) is relatively small. As a consequence, when immigration is keenly contested in national politics, those institutions have only limited opportunities for discussion, negotiation, and bargaining with decision-makers. Short-term thinking prevails, with an eye on public opinion and electoral agendas. Today, in many immigration countries, the contradiction is not so much between the imperatives of economic liberalism and controlling borders, as it is between social solidarity and security.

Hollifield's recent research on displacement and the challenge of forced migration (2021) proposes a four-sided typology of migration governance, involving security, rights, markets, and culture.

2.4 Thomas Faist: The Transnational Social Question as an Alternative to Class Struggle at the Global Scale

Thomas Faist is Professor of Sociology at the University of Bielefeld, in Germany. He has pursued his work on transnationalism in migration through a large number of comparative studies. In his last book, *The Transnational Social Question* (2019), he focuses on transnationalism as a global challenge.

Transnationalism was introduced as a category of analysis in migration studies by Linda Basch and Nina Glick Schiller (1994) in the early 1990s, in a period when the role of nation states as the main actors in both the national and the international order was being challenged. Some political scientists and sociologists, such as Bertrand Badie and Saskia Sassen, used this concept to speak of the decline of nation states and the increasing role of global cities (Sassen, 1996), the emergence of new actors in the Global South (Badie, 2009), and of the new role of associations as important actors in international arenas. Other observers studied transnationalism using a bottom-up analysis, emphasising that transnational practices were being developed by migrant diasporas and the influence of countries of origin (through "the strength of weak ties", as Mark Granoveter puts it; 1973) as a way of circumventing the rules imposed by nation states rules or in order to transgress borders (Dufoix, 2003; Soysal, 1994; on transnational citizenship, see Bauböck, 1994).

Thomas Faist's book *The Transnational Social Question* analyses migration with a new lens. He does not use the concept of transnationalism in the manner described above: the concept now extends more broadly to transborder mobility, remittances, the transborder migration of work, and the dissemination of ways of life. One of the strongest ideas developed by Thomas Faist lies in his demonstration that class struggles inside one country, particularly those in an industrial context (as conceived by Marx), now generally play a lesser role than social inequalities between countries of the Global North and Global South. The book explores the whole, complex migration system through this transnational approach to social questions.

Thomas Faist has developed two useful concepts for analysing migration from the perspective of social transnationalism:

- The dominant theoretical paradigm for analysing migration is no longer that of internal class struggle (within countries), but that of social and cultural inequalities between the Global South and the Global North. These inequalities create asymmetric regimes across the world, leading to migration, and "exit" rather than "voice", according to Alfred Hirschman's book *Exit, Voice and Loyalty* (1970). Now conflicts are less dominated by internal class struggles than they are by heterogeneities (religious, ethnic, linguistic, etc.) between states viewed through the North-South prism.
- Location (where you were born and where you are currently living) has become the most important factor in heterogeneity and inequality. The world has passed from a model of class difference to one characterised by differences of place and citizenship. The place where you were born now gives rise to the greatest inequalities, since your future, your right to mobility, and your access to social rights are all linked to your passport. In some cases, you may be perceived as representing a "migration risk", and consequently you will not be able to travel without a visa. Furthermore, human insecurity and forced migration are linked to the Global South, where there is a far greater prevalence of failed states and civil war. Most migrants are looking for social protection, gender and sexual equality, access to education, health, and water. It is not the poorest people who leave their countries, since such people lack access to transnational networks (family, friends, money, language skills), but rather those who are more educated and informed, and who are thus more aware that they can seek a better future outside their countries of origin. In a turbulent context, they are looking for more security (political, social, economic, health-related). They therefore send large amounts of remittances – a practice that is made possible thanks to migration. They may also build transnational mobilisations focused on addressing social inequalities.

With a transnational and global approach, access to social protection appears as a major divide between the Global North and Global South. Social welfare policies can either include or exclude non-nationals. In reality, many migrants, as a result of their choice of mobility, do not have any formal status in their country of residence, and are therefore excluded from all forms of citizenship and access to social rights. Some of them acquire a few rights, either through humanitarian protection policies or legalisation, but this is often a temporary situation.

At the international level, no international organisation has the ambition to reduce inequalities in the provision of social protection between states. They are active only inside countries, in spite of the very heterogeneous landscape of social protection. There is no coherent global migration regime, and the systems of global migration governance do not deal with international social inequalities and heterogeneities. Border controls exclude some categories from any social protection, leading to further deaths. Diasporas are addressing some of these issues of social care and welfare in such globally inter-connected nations as the US, Canada, and Australia, by creating networks of support and advocacy. Environmental changes could also increase some migration flows in response to inequalities in some parts of the world, mostly by creating differences in vulnerabilities between regions of departure and arrival.

In the last 10 years, heterogeneities (ethnic, religious, linguistic) have become stronger between countries of emigration and immigration across the North-South divide. These heterogeneities are transnational in nature, involving transborder migratory patterns, remittances, recruitment, and the dissemination of different ways of life. The modern political world is increasingly characterised by economic and political inequalities. Inequalities between countries are greater than inequalities within nation states. Transborder migration has become externalised with the use of bilateral and multilateral agreements.

Another inequality lies in the rural/urban gap, which is accelerating the rapid transition from a model of class difference to one based on one's location in the world and access to social protection. Citizenship is linked with location. The weakness of some political regimes in the world leads to a lack of governmental capabilities in those states (which is itself a factor in international migration), human security concerns, and forced migration due to civil wars and the collapse of states. Many sovereign countries are effectively dominated in the international order. Global economic inequalities and asymmetries of power, which are maintained in order to support the rule of law and the legal use of violence, lead to migration. Countries that do not succeed in protecting themselves from inequalities and violence are likely to create flows of refugees. Many migrants are motivated by the search for social protection, and proceed to make up for inequalities with the use of remittances and transfers of information regarding health and care services. Women's rights, and the search for equality, security, education, and water are all often stronger factors for departure than poverty alone. In these countries we can observe political mobilisations and transnational movements fighting against social inequalities.

Migration reinforces the crucial importance of one's place of origin and place of residence as the most significant factor for one's conditions of living and future prospects. In a period when location is more important than one's place on the human development index, there are paradoxically fewer possibilities for international migration than in earlier periods, owing to the emergence of new inequalities in the right to migrate, linked to visa regimes and border controls. Consequently, a transnationalisation from below is developing, and the unequal right to migrate is becoming an important factor in the hierarchical structuring of heterogeneities. This situation is leading to a situation of selective mobility and massive immobility, in which we can observe a global hierarchy of inequality with many intersectional factors (class, gender, ethnicity, race, religion, citizenship). The transnational social question is now both global and local.

2.5 Aristide Zolberg: "The Main Gate and the Back Door", "Strange Bedfellows", and the Influence of External Factors on the Internal Political Order

After growing up in Belgium during the Second World War, Aristide Zolberg decided to migrate to the US. When he acquired American citizenship, he served in the army, which gave him the opportunity to travel to Africa. After completing a PhD on Francophone Africa, he became a professor of political science at the University of Chicago, then at the New School for Social Research in New York. He was one of the first political scientists to analyse migration from an international perspective, through his work on borders, refugees, and comparative immigration policies, mainly between France and the US. In 1985, he analysed the effect of migration on the relation between the national and the international political orders, in terms of influence and intrusion, mostly in connection with transnational diasporas (Zolberg, 1985). In his last book, *A Nation by Design* (2006), his analysis of the role of immigration in the making of the US led him to develop the concept of "the main gate and the back door", referring to the choice faced by migrants between legal or irregular migratory routes into an immigration country with strong border controls. He also observed the heterogeneity of actors who support migrant populations, which he describes as "strange bedfellows". This heterogeneity weakens transnational mobilisations advocating for changes in migration policies: emigration countries, employers, and associations of undocumented migrants are in favour of more open borders, but these groups do not have a tradition of fighting together for a common cause, whereas immigration countries, welfare countries, and nationalists are consistent in their opposition to increased access for immigrants. He also showed very early on the role of refugees in the internationalisation of issues of migration (Zolberg et al., 1989).

Among many other well-known political scientists and sociologists who have addressed migration as an international issue, we could point to the work of Didier Bigo and Elspeth Guild on the concepts of the externalisation of borders and the use of buffer zones with control and readmission agreements (2005), Robin Cohen on diasporas as a factor in transnationalisation (2008, 2018), and Stephen Vertovec on transnationalism (2004).

2.5.1 II – Historical Overview

The history of mass migration began in the nineteenth century, when revolutions across Europe, poverty, the exclusion of minorities, labour shortages, and demands for the settlement of populations in empty territories or places of colonisation led to the movement of millions of people to new destinations. Most countries of departure were powerful (the "Great Empires") while most countries of destination were weak and colonised (the US, Canada, Australia, Algeria). The land itself was attractive, offering the prospect of the construction of a New World (in North and South America, Australia, and New Zealand). The modernisation of sea transportation in the mid-nineteenth century, with the transition from boats driven by the wind to steam boats capable of carrying large numbers of passengers, is another technical and powerful factor of mass migration. Migrants left for settlement or for work, even though most people leaving for settlement eventually returned home (such as the 20 million Italian migrants to the Americas who later returned to Italy), while some who moved for work ultimately decided to stay (mostly in Europe).

Unlike other migration destinations, Europe never considered itself as an immigration continent of settlement, since, during the nineteenth century, most migrants were European, and owing to its large population Europe was overall an emigration continent. The only exception was France, which began its demographic decline at the end of the eighteenth century and became an immigration country (in order to compensate for labour shortages). Meanwhile, other European countries remained emigration countries, including migration to France, but also to other destination. For example, Germans, Poles, Italians, Spaniards, and Portuguese travelled both to France and to the Americas.

During the twentieth century, the First and Second World wars created new demands for labour for reconstruction, while the collapse of Great Empires (the Ottoman Empire, Russia, Austria-Hungary) led to new flows of refugees and minorities to Europe (including exchanges of populations, such as those between Greece and Turkey) and to North and South America. After the Second World War, the creation of new borders in Eastern Europe led to the movement of 12 million people, mostly ethnic Germans leaving lands that had become Poland or the Czech Republic to travel to destinations within the new borders of Germany. In the following years, a period of economic growth (1945–1974) transformed former emigration countries in Europe into immigration countries (the UK, Germany, Switzerland, the Benelux states). At the start of the 1980s, Southern European countries also became immigration countries (Italy, Spain, Portugal, Greece), having formerly been emigration countries. In the 1990s, the fall of the Iron Curtain gave rise to new flows of migration: these included ethnic movements of population from the former USSR to Germany (2 million "Aussiedler"), and the disentanglement of populations in Eastern and Central Europe (such as those between the Czech Republic and Slovakia, and between Romania and Hungary, and the movement of Greeks from the north of the Black Sea to Greece, and of Bulgarians of Muslim culture to Turkey). The enlargement of the EU in 2004 with the entry of ten new countries led to these populations – formerly enclosed within strong borders – becoming commuters between EU Member States: many workers adopted mobility as a way of life, facilitated by the relatively short distances between countries of work and of origin. We can therefore identify four main periods of major migration movements in European countries during the twentieth century: first, immigration to France, dating back to the mid-nineteenth century; next, immigration to Germany, the UK, Benelux, and the Nordic countries after the Second World War (and throughout the mid-twentieth century); from the 1980s, Southern Europe became an immigration region; and Eastern Europe became involved in large-scale migration from the early 1990s.

In the twenty-first century, a new era of mobility and migration between the Global North and the Global South was initiated by several factors: the transformation of some Southern countries into immigration countries owing to their dependence on migrant workers (notably the Gulf states, since the rise in oil prices from 1973 onwards), the growing divide between richer and poorer countries in the Global South, and South-South movements of refugees. 75% of refugees from countries in the Global South (notably Afghans, Iraqis, Syrians, Sudanese, and Sub-Saharans from the Great Lakes region) travelled to other Southern countries (Iran and Pakistan for Afghans, Lebanon for refugees from Middle Eastern countries, Turkey for Syrians, and Egypt and Uganda for Sudanese). Environmentally displaced persons were also involved in South-South migration, mostly at the internal level, but partly (roughly a third) at the international level, to neighbouring countries. Some countries in the Global South, such as Lebanon, Turkey, and those on the southern rim of the Mediterranean Sea (Algeria, Tunisia, Morocco, and Libya), also became transit countries, owing to their geographical position between North and South.

Many of these flows are mixed, in terms of the economic and political profiles of individual migrants. The reasons for this are historical. In most immigration countries in the Global North, migration policies moved from an orientation towards the socio-economic management of workers to a security-based approach to the management of borders. In the mid-1950s, the main categories of migrants were workers (who made up the majority), followed by families and refugees. Migration policies in Western Europe were mainly determined by the economic need to compensate for labour shortages, rather than in response to families and refugees, who made up a minority of migrants. Migrant workers were not seen as future settlers, and those who arrived by irregular channels were rapidly legalised in their status, since they were required as legal workers. There was no confusion between workers and refugees. At this time, refugees were welcomed, since they strengthened the image of Europe, the US, and Canada as Western countries of democracy and freedom, providing a safe haven to those who had been persecuted and threatened in countries in the Communist Bloc. The situation is now very different. Western European countries largely closed their borders to workers from around 1973–1974. Some migrants acquired European citizenship (through the Maastricht Treaty of 1992 on European Citizenship, article 8), with the right to free circulation that this entails (among the largest populations: Italians, Portuguese, Spaniards, Greeks, and later Poles and Romanians), while migrants from non-EU states were granted access using visas through the Schengen Agreement of 1985. These migrants were expected to return to their countries of origin, but in most cases this did not occur, and these migrant workers who had formerly been "required" increasingly became "undesirable" in their countries of destination. Meanwhile, the influence of Gulf countries on Muslim emigration countries led to changes in the practice of Islam at home and abroad, which were also affected by the international context (wars in Iraq and Afghanistan, flows of Palestinian refugees, the collapse of Libya after the "Arab

Springs" of 2011, the civil war in Syria, and terrorism in both emigration and immigration countries).

For young people in the Global South, the possibility of migrating through irregular channels by means of human smugglers, and the portrayal in the media of Europe, the US, and Canada as an Eldorado, are contributing to a desire to emigrate. For those who undertake these often dangerous journeys, without any passport or visa, the only prospect for obtaining a legal status is by claiming asylum. They therefore politicise their identities, even if they are not in reality persecuted in their country of origin. This leads to "mixed flows", blurring the boundaries between those who travel for work and those who require asylum because, for example, civil war is destroying their country. However, the likelihood of such migrants being recognised as refugees is much lower than it was during the Cold War. Many of them, having been refused refugee status, join the flow of irregular migrants, seeking and finding work on the black market. In the past, 90% of those who sought refugee status were successful in their claims (notably in the 1950s and, for Vietnamese and Chileans, in the 1980s), but now 60% of claims for asylum are refused. The same phenomenon of blurred profiles is found in the case of family reunification: most migrants in this category travel to join a family member already working in Europe, but then also themselves enter the labour market. The difference between migration of settlement and labour migration is therefore blurred, as well as that between forced and voluntary migration. The same phenomenon can be observed once again with regard to students, who enter a country of destination to study, but subsequently enter the labour force.

In the past, most migrants found themselves housed in slums, or in collective housing for workers ("foyers" in France), or named "Gastarbeiter" (Germany, Benelux), who were explicitly expected to work but not to remain for settlement. The closure of borders to labour migration in the mid-1970s led to an increase in settlement through family reunification. Whereas European migrants could come and go freely, borders were increasingly closed to non-EU nationals, and their perceived illegitimacy increased as unemployment grew in European countries.

In the early 1980s, following the rise in oil prices, Gulf countries began to have enough money to subsidise Muslim associations, building prayer rooms in migrants' countries of origin, and in Europe influencing the landscape of migrant districts, where headscarves, libraries, halal butchers, and Muslim clothes were increasingly visible. At a time when the opposition between the West and the Communist Bloc had ceased to represent the greatest division in the global order, Muslims became the new enemies (Huntington, 1993).

Migration gradually came to be perceived and treated as a security issue. In Brussels, with the Treaty of Amsterdam of 1997, migration passed from being a socio-economic concern to being a question of justice and internal affairs. In EU Member States, migration was no longer the concern of ministries in charge of work and social issues, but rather ministries of the interior, or even of defence or justice (as in the Nordic countries). In the 1990s and 2000s, migration came to be seen as a military confrontation in the Mediterranean, to be addressed using the tools of the Schengen Information System (created in 2000) and Frontex (created in 2004).

Other changes in attitudes towards migration can be observed in the change in the use of language, such as the shift from terms of "assimilation", to "integration", and then to questions of "living together". Various models have been adopted across Europe, including forms of "multiculturalism" in the UK, Germany, and Benelux, and a debate in France between principles of social cohesion (as espoused by Jacques Chirac in 1995) or separatism (a term promoted by Emmanuel Macron in 2020). Southern European countries (Italy, Spain, Portugal, Greece) have not defined a clear philosophy, as they more recently became immigration countries, with the attendant questions of legalising irregular migrants and managing increasingly stratified labour markets.

In Germany, the use of the term "Leitkultur" (a supposedly shared culture of modern, essentially liberal-democratic values) implied that migrants did not possess such values from their own cultural background. Meanwhile anti-migrant movements were rising across Europe, centred on a number of themes and narratives: those of the supposed Islamisation of Europe (AfD in Germany), the demographic shift from (white) Europeans to non-Europeans (referred to in French as the "grand remplacement"), the perceived failures of integration or of "multikulti" (as declared by Angela Merkel), the need to defend national identities, and perceived threats to security and borders (the far right Lega party in Italy). Far right political parties draw most of their arguments from these themes. Another stage in the development of such anti-migrant sentiment was reached in 2015, with the so-called "refugee crisis", when the claimed values of Europe (human rights, social solidarity, hospitality) came to be manifestly undermined by the sovereignism asserted by many nation states, and the refusal to welcome refugees in some European countries.

Since the 1980s, immigration policies have become politically symbolic, and have more often been orientated towards public opinion and the rise of the far right than towards effective migration management. In France, the National Front (now "Rassemblement National", or National Rally) made the issue of immigration control into its main topic for political campaigning. Many laws and policy discussions, such as the recurring debate around the granting of citizenship based on either *jus soli* (based on place of birth) or *jus sanguinis* (based on ancestry), have been brought about by the far right. As for entry laws, despite the increasing securitisation of borders, these measures have not succeeded in their aims of reducing flows of irregular migration, encouraging return to countries of origin, or promoting resettlement, although these three targets are present in almost all recent immigration laws and international summits. Most of these policies were highly mediatised, with a focus on demonstrating that they took into account some of the demands of the far right, rather than asserting that they would have effective outcomes.

The role of some counterbalances and pressure groups, such as high courts of justice and civic associations, can also undermine the war against migrants waged by the governments of some immigration countries. Some associations, such as the RESF (Réseau Education sans Frontières) since 2007, have been very successful in fighting against repatriations of families with children at school, while anti-discrimination associations have managed to increase diversity in public institutions and politics at the European scale. Many high courts, such as the Conseil

Constitutionnel and Conseil d'État in France (ruling on constitutional and administrative matters respectively), the European Court for Human Rights in Strasburg, and the Court of Justice of the European Union in Luxemburg show how judges and EU institutions can challenge the power of nation states. While national governments attempt to reassure public opinion that they maintain sovereignty over their borders, in some respects decision are taken elsewhere, either in Brussels or in Luxemburg. The result of such a highly mediatised policy-making process, turned towards public opinion, is that decisions are also determined by short-term electoral decision-making. Thus, after a long period in which migration policies were led by the economic need to compensate for labour shortages, they came to be dominated by public opinion and security issues, which are rarely conducive to a rational approach to migration management.

Historically, Europe was a continent of intense emigration, sending millions of its natives all over the world through labour emigration, colonisation, trade, missions, wars, and cooperation. In the 1960s Europe became a land of immigration, but both perceptions and politics related to migration seem to lag behind statistical and demographic facts.

In Europe, cooperation on migration management led to the harmonisation of migration policies – notably the externalisation of European border control – through the Schengen visa system from 1985 and bilateral and multilateral agreements with countries of origin. This led in turn to a reduction of opportunities for entry and the strengthening of military forms of border control and closure. This focus on closure in a world on the move can appear paradoxical. Waging a war on migration has produced a wide range of adverse effects, such as the creation of new criminal actors (human smugglers and traffickers), new migration routes (the Balkan route and the southern route through Niger and Libya), and abuses of human rights (particularly in the so-called "Libyan Hell").

In the wake of some terrorist murders committed by Islamic extremists, debates on sharing the burden of receiving refugees from Syria, Iraq, and the Horn of Africa have led to contradictory and confused claims about European borders. In particular, while refugees have sometimes been presented in a positive light as people to be saved, migrants have usually been viewed overall as people to be stopped, even though, in the new international context, refugees are a category of migrants.

Faced with the crisis of managing growing numbers of refugees, a gap appeared between, on the one hand, EU institutions, which insisted on principles of human rights (such as asylum and solidarity), and on the other hand, nation states, who focused their discourses and policies on the challenge that the new arrivals posed to the integrity of their national identities, notably in Eastern Europe. Central and Eastern European countries refused the proposal of the President of the European Commission Jean-Claude Juncker in 2015 to share the burden of resettlement. The member states of the Visegrad group (Hungary, the Czech Republic, Slovakia, and Poland) closed their national borders to newcomers, while in Germany Angela Merkel declared on September 2015 that Germany would welcome 800,000 refugees from Syria. Western European countries accepted the proposal by the European

Commission to institute quotas for the resettlement of asylum seekers, but these countries did not in practice receive large numbers of refugees for resettlement.

2.6 The Italian Crisis as a Case Study

Southern Italy has received large numbers of migrants rescued from the sea since the early 1990s. It has now become the third immigration country in Europe, after Germany and the UK, whereas France ranks fifth in terms of the number of foreigners on its territory. Just after the collapse of the Iron Curtain in 1991, the boats arriving in Puglia carried mainly Albanians. Ten years later, the arrivals were mostly from Africa, travelling via Libya and Tunisia. These included Sub-Saharans who had been smuggled across borders, and later some asylum seekers from the "Arab Springs" of 2011. Italy had previously concluded agreements with Libya for the repatriation of these migrants in exchange for the construction of infrastructure projects (such as a road from Egypt to Tunisia), but the political chaos that followed the fall of Gadhafi increased the numbers of human smugglers. Many Sub-Saharans arrived in Italy from Niger, via Libya. The most well-known episode from this period was the decision of the Italian Government of Enrico Letta, following the refusal of Frontex in October 2013 to lead a search and rescue operation after the wreckage of a boat with 400 people on board, to lead the operation "Mare Nostrum" to save victims lost at sea. 146,000 people were saved in 1 year from October 2013 to October 2014. Italy then entrusted this task to Triton, one of the operations of Frontex in the Mediterranean Sea. In spite of an undertaking to publicly manage the reception of migrants, which transferred many tasks to private NGOs and Catholic associations, such as Caritas in the south of the country, Italy had the feeling of being abandoned by Europe, owing to the indifference and selfishness of most other European countries.

After March 2016, the EU-Turkish agreement, which had mainly been concluded by Angela Merkel and individual EU Member States rather than by the EU, brought an end to the large numbers of arrivals from Syria through Greece, but this had the effect of further increasing arrivals in Europe through Italy. The Dublin 2 agreements on asylum (the "one-stop shop" system), according to which asylum seekers must register in the first European country in which they arrive, and then be examined as applicants in that country, increased the burden of arrivals in all southern European countries, and above all Italy, owing to its proximity to Tunisia and Libya, from which human smugglers operate sea crossings. A report of the Department of Human Rights of the United Nations in autumn 2017 focused attention on the "Libyan Hell" in particular, highlighting practices of slavery, human rights violations, prostitution, and extra-judicial imprisonment. The electoral success of the far right Lega party in May 2018, which allowed it to create a national government in coalition with another populist party, created a French-Italian crisis around the reception and rescuing of migrant boats. The episodes in which the Aquarius and other boats were prevented from landing on Mediterranean coasts in June 2018, together with the closure of the French-Italian border at Ventimiglia (near the French city of Nice) to newcomers from Africa arriving via Italy, revealed once again the lack of solidarity between European countries, both in terms of North-South and East-West relations, and the lack of trust of these countries towards EU proposals to relocate newcomers to all European countries. A break between Eastern and Western Europe continues to undermine European values of solidarity and human rights, and these values are being further challenged by the arguments of far right parties in all countries, including Hungary, Poland, and Austria.

2.6.1 III – 2015: The Challenge of Asylum for Europe

Europe had typically seen the arrival of between 200,000 and 400,000 asylum seekers per year before 2015, when this figure shot up to 1.2 million. However, the number of arrivals has decreased since 2015. We must remember that this crisis is not as new as many people suppose, since, after the fall of the Berlin Wall, Europe received 500,000 asylum seekers every year between 1989 to 1993, mostly in Germany, which received three-quarters of all asylum seekers in Europe. In 1995, the crisis in the former Yugoslavia also led to large numbers of refugees, most of whom arrived in Germany.

Present flows of refugees are mainly coming from Syria (6.5 million Syrians have left their country since 2013, and 7 million are internal refugees within Syria), Iraq (4 million), the Horn of Africa (travelling via Libya), Afghanistan (4 million), and Kosovo. Turkey has received the largest proportion of these refugees, with 4.5 million on its territory. This situation has led to conflict between EU Member States and EU institutions as to the best way to respond to the influx of migrants.

2.7 Conflict Between EU Member States and EU Institutions

The first answer offered at the European level, through the voice of Jean-Claude Juncker, President of the European Commission, was the proposal on May 2015 to share the burden of receiving refugees across the EU. During summer 2015, many central European countries closed their national borders to newcomers arriving along the Balkan route. Hungary was the first country to express its opposition to receiving new refugees, followed by the Czech Republic, Slovakia, and Poland – all countries in which far right parties were prominent in national politics. On September 2015, Jean-Claude Juncker made a new appeal to EU Member States to each welcome 160,000 asylum seekers. Angela Merkel's announcement on 7 September that Germany would receive 800,000 asylum seekers in 2015, closely followed by the widely shared photograph of the corpse of the three-year-old Syrian Aylan Kurdi, who washed ashore near Bodrum after the wreckage of the boat taken by his parents, led Western European states to accept, with some reluctance, Juncker's proposals. During 2015, according to UNHCR, Greece received the largest share of newcomers, who then tried to enter other EU Member States. Italy, who had received the largest numbers of arrivals before 2015, was also heavily involved, since the EU-Turkish agreements of March 2016 stopped most sea crossings between Turkey and Greece.

This agreement belongs to a long tradition of EU Member States bypassing the rules of their shared EU policies by means of bi- or multilateral agreements with non-European neighbour countries. The EU-Turkish agreement is thus the result of a number of negotiations between European nation states, led by Germany, and Turkey, rather than an EU treaty that would comply with EU norms. Libya was previously the most important contractor for European countries such as France and Italy, and played a role as a filter for Sub-Saharans wanting to reach Europe. President Gadhafi was paid with money, infrastructure projects, and recognition as a legitimate partner in return for his cooperation in the dirty job of containment and readmission. As Libya is now a land of human smugglers facilitating irregular migration, Turkey has instead become the co-contractor of choice for EU Member States. Through these agreements, Turkey came to be automatically considered as a safe country for asylum seekers. In return for its cooperation, it drove a hard bargain: €6 billion, the renewal of negotiations around Turkey's application to join the EU, and the removal of the requirement for visas for Turkish people visiting Europe. In fact, Turkish citizens represent the largest population of non-Europeans in the EU (4.5 million), although there are fewer Turks travelling from Turkey to Europe than there are returning from Europe to Turkey. The legitimacy of President Erdoğan, who had been criticised for his authoritarian rule and religious governance, was partly restored in the EU through these agreements. His re-election as President of Turkey reassured European states that Turkey would continue to be able to receive 4 million refugees under his leadership, while Europe itself remained unable to find a clear and united solution.

2.8 Factors of Failure and Implications for EU Member States and Institutions

Since 1990, EU immigration and asylum policies have focused on a security-based approach, using the tools of dissuasion, repression, and confinement. The Schengen system of reinforcing control of Europe's external borders led to thousands of people dying in the Mediterranean Sea between 2000 and 2020. Since 2015, 4000 people have died at sea every year. The main response to the closure of borders is the emergence of human smuggling, which provides large sums of money to smugglers, with limited possibilities for restricting those involved. Nonetheless, after every disaster at sea, the Frontex mechanism (established in 2004 as a shared police force at the EU's external borders, and implemented from 2005) saw its funding increased, without questions as to its effectiveness. From €5 million in 2004, it budget has now reached €500 million. The Dublin agreements on asylum have been criticised but never abandoned: the Dublin I (1990) agreement tried to define a common EU asylum policy to combat "asylum shopping", thus reducing individuals' chances of getting refugee status through a harmonisation of policies between all EU Member States. Dublin II (2003), which was highly criticised but never cancelled, asserts that an asylum seeker who has entered an EU Member State must make a claim for asylum in that country (the "one-stop shop" system). In practice this system does not work, because asylum seekers usually have a precise idea of the country where they want to apply, and Greece is rarely their first choice. The European strategy of extending its war on irregular migration to the southern rim of the Mediterranean also runs into difficulties, owing to the sovereignty of countries of departure on the North African coast, as well as the difficulty of preventing clandestine departures from their coasts. Both return policies and dissuasion policies have shown their limited effectiveness, and yet have repeatedly been proposed anew.

However, the greatest failure is the crisis of solidarity between EU Member States. In the years before Dublin II, the approach proposed by most large countries of destination for asylum seekers – such as Germany and Austria in the wake of the fall of the Berlin wall – was that of sharing the burden across the EU. The Dublin II regime effectively placed most of the burden on Southern European countries with a Mediterranean coast, and especially Italy and Greece. A divergence also appeared in 2015 between Eastern and Western European countries regarding EU proposals for resettlement: most Eastern European countries refused to receive newcomers and closed their national borders, on the grounds that large numbers of immigrants would undermine the integrity of their national identity and increase the risk of terrorist attacks. However, solidarity is one of the values of the EU, as defined in the EU Treaty of Lisbon, and is also one of the founding values of the EU, alongside democracy, the protection of human rights, liberalism, diversity, and the secularisation of the state. The challenges of immigration and refugee policy have given rise to a lack of trust between EU Member States, connected to the rise of nationalist ideologies all over Europe and the return of national borders and assertions of state sovereignty.

Other possible solutions were not debated, such as the possibility of implementing a 2001 European directive on temporary protection for newcomers who do not fit the criteria of refugees as defined by the Geneva Convention, or the creation of legal channels for immigration for employment. The continuing use of old solutions that have repeatedly proven their ineffectiveness, such as return policies and repatriation agreements (which formed part of the Valletta Euro-African summit of autumn 2015, and then the European summit of June 2018 in Brussels), are also part of the crisis, which is ultimately more a crisis of solidarity than of refugees themselves.

2.9 Civil Society and "Crimes of Solidarity", Ethics Versus Control

Over the course of this long migration crisis, new civil society actors have emerged to defend the rights of migrants: NGOs, associations focused on migrants' rights (PICUM at the EU level, Caritas, CIMADE, and GISTI in France), and human rights associations (Amnesty International, Ligue des droits de l'Homme). Some associations (Utopia 56, No Border in Calais) have been considered as activists, and their members have been interrogated intensively by the police. Some individuals have been prosecuted and found guilty of breaking national laws. In France, Cédric Herrou, a farmer in the south-east of France was prosecuted for providing support to irregular migrants whom he welcomed at his farm: these were Sub-Saharan Africans who had got lost in the mountains trying to cross the border between Italy and France. The 2018 film *Free* relates the true story of this journey. Other films have been produced on this subject, mostly highlighting the contradictions between the law and humane ethical principles: *Terra ferma* and *Fuocoammare* about Lampedusa, and *L'escale* about Greece. There are also many books on similar subjects. In southern Italy, the mayor of Riace, Domenico Lucani, was prohibited from staying in the town where he was the mayor because he provided jobs to irregular migrants in a cooperative. Some well-known mayors, such as Leoluca Orlando, mayor of Palermo (subsequently re-elected with 72% of the vote), refused to abide by the law requiring the closure of harbours, and continued to receive newcomers during the period when the far right party Lega was part of the national government in 2018. The situation was similar for Damien Carême, the ecologist mayor of Grande-Synthe, in the north of France, close to Calais and Dunkirk.

In recent years, the principal contradiction has no longer been that between economic liberalism and the control of borders, but rather that between solidarity and security. After Cédric Herrou was repeatedly prosecuted for his role in assisting irregular migrants attempting to enter France, the Conseil constitutionnel – the highest court in France – judged in summer 2018 that his actions were admissible on the basis that such actions of "fraternity" (one of the founding values of the French Republic, alongside freedom and equality) are protected by the Constitution. This judgement put an end to his prosecution.

2.10 Dilemmas Between Wisdom and Politics: Public Opinion and Decision-Making

On migration issues, the gap between knowledge and political decision-making continues. For the social sciences, the analysis of ongoing events is difficult, without the benefit of the distance that makes research possible. Yet it is precisely in times of crisis that scientific knowledge, and particularly policy-relevant data and analyses, are sought after. The overall trends of European migration policy in the past decades appear to be at odds with the main results of scientific knowledge

2.10 Dilemmas Between Wisdom and Politics: Public Opinion and Decision-Making

gathered around migration issues in the last 30 years by researchers and experts. This includes not only findings from academic circles but also those from governmental and non-governmental organisations. The gap between knowledge on migration matters and the perceptions involved in policy making is part of a more general gap between science and politics. While this divergence is not new, it is particularly acute for the case of migration and refugee policies in the EU. This gap poses some serious questions. Why do EU Member States tend not to anticipate refugee crises (either now, or in the early 1990s when refugees fled the Caucasus region and the Balkans), and conversely, why do they anticipate crises that do not happen (for example, after the demise of the Soviet Union and the fall of the Berlin wall)? Why do policy makers stick to decisions and policy options that have manifestly failed to achieve their explicit goals in the past?

Migration studies specialists have suggested that migration is a field where policy inefficiency is particularly striking, and have named this the "gap hypothesis". Stephen Castles, among others, has also theorised the "failure" of migration policies and the discrepancy between the desired control of migration flows and the difficulties of absorbing migrants into the populations of developed countries. The theme of "migration policy failure" has yet again come to the fore, with recent migration, asylum, and humanitarian "crises" in the Mediterranean. Yet, for specialists in the field, the current "crisis" has mostly been interpreted as a continuation of long-term mechanisms and trends rather than as an abrupt change (Schmoll et al., 2015).

One can argue that migration policies fail because policy makers do not listen to the "wise" advice of researchers and experts, and fail to explore the various reasons for such failure (public opinion, short-term economic interests, institutional path dependency, etc.). We can also analyse and question the ways in which migration knowledge is produced and disseminated among policy circles. Since most governing institutions, and the EU in particular, claim to construct policy agendas on the basis of scientific evidence, we can explore the processes through which migration specialists (academics, experts, and activists) are involved in (or excluded from) policy making. The importance of expertise and science in European policy cycles is often highlighted in policy documents and roadmaps, such as in this passage from a white paper in 2001: "scientific and other experts play an increasingly significant role in preparing and monitoring decisions. From human and animal health to social legislation, the institutions rely on specialist expertise to anticipate and identify the nature of problems and uncertainties that the Union faces, to take decisions and to ensure risks can be explained clearly and simply to the public" (European Commission, 2001, p. 19). However, the decision-making process makes it difficult to diverge from the path dependency established by older frameworks of EU migration policies, including those which did not succeed in their goals, because the veto of one country can block any attempt at change.

At the global level, faced with the failure of most immigration policies, countries in the Global South are now part of the debate and are beginning to make their voice heard in World Social Forums, as well in the annual meetings of the Global Forum on Migration and Development (GFMD) and the United Nations High Level Dialogue on Migration and Development (UN-HLD).

2.11 Conclusion

The current situation of migration and migration governance leaves a wide range of questions unresolved, including: the situation of the 13 million stateless people in the world, environmentally displaced persons without any status, and the unexpected consequences on migration flows of phenomena such as the fluctuating price of cotton, the development of coffee plantations in new countries such as Vietnam, extensive fishing in African waters by Chinese or Japanese vessels, and changes to volatile markets in raw materials. These problems and developments demonstrate the interdependency of migration in relation to other global concerns, yet migration policy continues to be dominated by assertions of sovereignty by nation states and the intense politicisation of the topic.

Migration is one of the most controversial topics in public policy, because it includes a large number of unspoken contradictions: between economic liberalism and security-based approaches to dissuading and restricting migration, between human rights and state controls, between economic and demographic needs and nationalist attempts to close borders, between ethics and sovereignty, and between mobility and development. In the current migration regime, mobility inevitably gives rise to the transgression of laws and borders. And in a world on the move, the nation state stands to lose the most, because the stability of borders, populations, identity, citizenship, and the rule of national laws are all challenged by transnational and liquid forms of movement (Wihtol de Wenden, 2017a, b).

References

Badie, B. (2009). *Puissant ou solidaire? Principes d'humanisme international*. Desclée de Bouwer.
Bauböck, R. (1994). *Transnational citizenship: Membership and rights in international migration*. Edward Elgar.
Bigo, D., & Guild, E. (2005). *Controlling frontiers: Free movement into or within Europe*. Ashgate.
Bretell, C., & Hollifield, J. (2014). *Migration theory: Talking across disciplines*. Routledge.
Castles, S., & Davidson, A. (2000). *Citizenship and migration: Globalisation and the politics of belonging*. Macmillan.
Castles, S., De Haas, H., & Miller, M. (2014). *The age of migration: International movements of population in the modern world*. Macmillan.
Cohen, R. (2008). *Global diasporas, an introduction*. Routledge.
Comte, E. (2018). *The history of the European migration regime: Germany's strategic hegemony*. Routledge.
Dufoix, S. (2003). *Les diasporas*. Presses Universitaires de France.
European Commission. (2001). *European governance: A white paper, Brussels 25/7/2001 COM(2001) 428 final*. European Commission.
Faist, T. (2019). *The transnational social question*. Oxford University Press.
Granovetter, M. (1973). The strength of weak ties. *American Journal of Sociology, 78*(6), 1360–1380.
Hirschman, A. (1970). *Exit, voice and loyalty: Responses to decline in firms, organisations and states*. Harvard University Press.

References

Hollifield, J. (1992). *Immigration, markets and states: American policy and politics.* Harvard University Press.

Hollifield, J. (2021). Driven out: Displacement and the challenge of forced migration. *The Wilson Quarterly, 3* (special issue: Humanity in motion: Scenes from the global displacement crisis).

Huntington, S. (1993). The clash of civilisations. *Foreign Affairs, 72*(3), 22–49.

Sassen, S. (1996). *Losing control? Sovereignty in an age of globalisation.* Columbia University Press.

Schmoll, C., Thiollet, H., & Wihtol de Wenden, C. (2015). *Migrations en Méditerranée.* CNRS Editions.

Soysal, Y. (1994). *The limits of citizenship: Migrants and post-colonial citizenship in Europe.* Chicago University Press.

UNDESA Report. (2021). *UNDESA International migration report 2021.*

Vertovec, S. (2004). Migrant transnationalism and modes of transformation. *International Migration Review, 38,* 970–2001.

Wihtol de Wenden, C. (1988). *Les immigrés et la politique: Cent-cinquante ans d'évolution.* Presses de la FNSP.

Wihtol de Wenden, C. (2017a). *La question migratoire au XXIème siècle: Migrants, réfugiés et relations internationales.* Presses de Sciences Po.

Wihtol de Wenden, C. (2017b). *Faut-il ouvrir les frontières?* Presses de Sciences Po.

Zolberg, A. (1985). L'influence des facteurs externes sur l'ordre politique interne. In J. L. Jean & M. Grawitz (Eds.), *Traité de science politique.* Presses Universitaires de France.

Zolberg, A. (2006). *A nation by design: Immigration policy and the fashioning of America.* Cambridge University Press.

Zolberg, A., Suhrke, A., & Aguayo, S. (1989). *Escape from violence: Conflict and the refugee crisis in the developing world.* Oxford University Press.

Open Access This chapter is licensed under the terms of the Creative Commons Attribution 4.0 International License (http://creativecommons.org/licenses/by/4.0/), which permits use, sharing, adaptation, distribution and reproduction in any medium or format, as long as you give appropriate credit to the original author(s) and the source, provide a link to the Creative Commons license and indicate if changes were made.

The images or other third party material in this chapter are included in the chapter's Creative Commons license, unless indicated otherwise in a credit line to the material. If material is not included in the chapter's Creative Commons license and your intended use is not permitted by statutory regulation or exceeds the permitted use, you will need to obtain permission directly from the copyright holder.

Chapter 3
Refugees

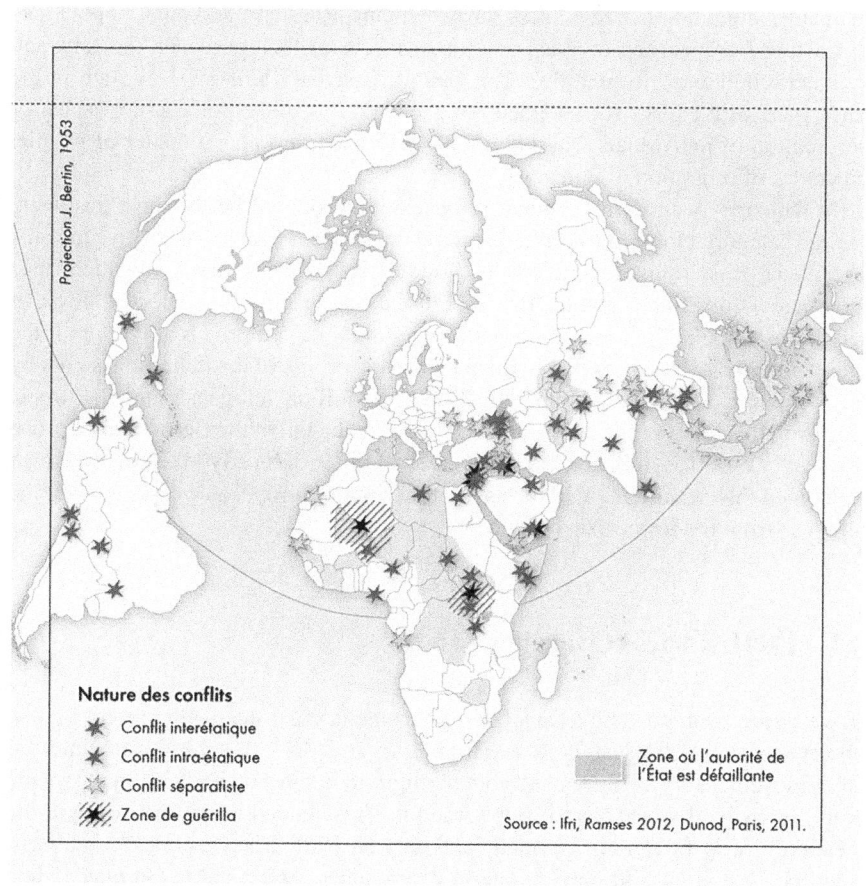

Refugees
Add Venezuela and Ukraine on the map
Source: UNHCR The State of Refugees in the World 2022

The management of refugees is perhaps the aspect of migration that has been most extensively viewed and approached from an international perspective. After a period when there was no public policy in place related to refugees, during which they were welcomed by churches and other private networks (such as French Protestants during the seventeenth century seeking refuge in Germany, the UK, and the Netherlands), and some individual elites went into exile in response to regime changes and revolutions (such as Chateaubriand, Louis Napoléon Bonaparte, and Victor Hugo, to mention the most well-known exiles from France), the topic became far more pressing on the international scene after the collapse of some of the Great Empires of the nineteenth century: the Russian Empire, the Ottoman Empire, and the Austrian-Hungarian Empire. The Nansen passport was created in 1922 in order to avoid a situation of statelessness for Armenians, Russians, and other populations of Eastern Europe, then to assist victims of fascism (the "fuorusciti" in Italy, and Spanish republicans from 1939). The Geneva Convention of 1951, written in the early years of the Cold War, defined refugees in terms of the persecution or fear of persecution of individuals, but definitions of refugees are now a matter of parallel processes of migration diplomacy.

In the early twenty-first century, refugees have come to be the most positively viewed category of migrants. Public opinion in Europe is also more positive towards so-called "good refugees" (from the Middle East) than towards so-called "bad migrants" (from Sub-Saharan Africa). Europe has faced unprecedented flows of refugees since 2015, and large flows of forced migration more broadly, even if the individuals in such "mixed flows" do not all fit the profile of the definition set out by the Geneva Convention of 1951. In 2015, 1.2 million refugees entered Europe. However, this crisis is not without precedent: after the fall of the Berlin Wall, Europe received 500,000 asylum seekers between 1989 to 1993, mostly in Germany, which welcomed three-quarters of all the asylum seekers to Europe, as well as most of the refugees from the former Yugoslavia.

3.1 I – Historical Overview

If we adopt a broad definition of refugees, including forced migration, we can observe that, over the last 70 years (from 1951 to 2021), the world has witnessed large movements of refugees and forced migration approximately every 20 years. After the Second World War, Europe faced flows of forced migration owing to the creation of new borders in Germany and an Iron Curtain between East and West. Between 12 and 14 million Germans ("Vertriebenen") returned to Germany when their land became Polish (in the regions of Gdańsk, Szczeczin, Poznań, and Wrocław), Russian (the oblast of Koenigsberg/Kaliningrad), and Czech (the Sudetenland). These were ethnic and forced migrants, but not refugees in the strict sense. Their former borders and countries had disappeared. Later, "Ubersiedler" tried to cross the Berlin Wall, built in 1961, and the Hungarian Revolution of 1956 brought asylum seekers to Western Europe, along with other dissenters from communist regimes in the USSR and Eastern Europe. These dissenters from the Communist Bloc fitted perfectly with the popular image of refugees: mostly well-educated, cosmopolitan intellectuals, leaving their countries with the hope of finding freedom in Western countries in Europe, the US, or Canada, and sociologically very different from the migrant workers of those times, who tended to be rural and uneducated, and intended to return to their countries of origin. Most of these asylum seekers attained refugee status without difficulty. However, the management of refugees was not a politicised issue in destination countries. Debates on migration were instead focused on the management of labour migration.

The 1970s witnessed the emergence of new political crises, with flows of exiles from various civil wars in Latin America, mainly travelling to the US and Canada, and of Vietnamese, Cambodian, and Laotian "boat people", who sought shelter in the US, Canada, and France. Public opinion in countries of destination was very positive towards these exiles, even if the political orientation of the newcomers was sometimes opposed (the Vietnamese tried to escape to communist regimes, while Chileans arriving in France in 1973 after the putsch of General Pinochet were leftist activists, who were warmly welcomed by French intellectuals). This second period of major flows of forced migration ends with the 1979 Iranian Revolution, and the arrival in Western Europe and the US of Iranian refugees fleeing the risk of religious radicalisation in the 1980s. These were also recognised as refugees, and most of them were received and without difficulties.

The 1990s marked a turning point. Firstly, the fall of the Iron Curtain and of the Berlin Wall created flows of ethnic migration (but not refugees) in a process of disentanglement of European nation states: 2 million "Aussiedler" arrived in Germany after 1989, mostly from Russia, the Baltic regions, Kazakhstan, and the regions around the Volga River (Saratov), and acquired German citizenship based on linguistic and cultural criteria; 500,000 Muslim Bulgarians, faced with religious discrimination, left their country for Turkey; Romanians in Transylvania, of Hungarian origin, returned to Hungary; and 350,000 Greeks from the north-east coast of the Black Sea (in the former USSR) returned to Greece. However, the largest flow of exiles of this period was the departure of Jewish Russians from the former USSR to Israel, which had an impact on Israeli society in terms of politics (the exiles were mostly right wing voters) and cultural balance (between Ashkenazi and Sephardic Jews). Some other conflicts, such as those in Lebanon, the African Great Lakes, and Eritrea, as well as the long Darfur crisis in Sudan, created flows of refugees, which were mostly South-South flows. From 1990 until the present, the reception of refugees has ceased to be practised as a demonstration of Western values in the face of repression by communist regimes. Countries of destination are faced with groups whose forced migrations are motivated by threats other than purely political ones: besides political activists, forced migrants may face persecution on the basis of religion, ethnic belonging, social class, and sexual identity or orientation.

The years 2011–2015 saw the emergence of the so-called Arab Springs, as well as some long-lasting conflicts which also gave rise to millions of refugees, notably those in Afghanistan (6.5 million from the end of the 1970s until now), Sri Lanka, Somalia, and Darfur. Most of these were received by neighbouring countries, in

South-South flows: Iran and Pakistan for Afghans, Chad and Egypt for Sudanese (Darfuri), and Syria and Lebanon for Iraqis. Northern Europe, the US, and Canada also received refugees from the Middle East (Lebanon, Iran, Iraq, Palestinians, and Kurds) and the Horn of Africa. The Syrian crisis, which was a consequence of a failed Arab Spring uprising in 2011, led to the departure of 5 million people, mostly families, while 7 million people were internally displaced within their country. Currently, Venezuela is the greatest source of exiles (4.5 million people, seeking asylum mainly in Colombia and Brazil, but also in Europe). The largest flows to Europe are those of Syrians, Afghans, Venezuelans, Colombians, Iraqis, and most recently Ukrainians. The countries receiving the largest numbers of forced migrants are Germany, France, and Spain. 84% of Syrian asylum seekers are granted refugee status, 80% of Eritreans, and 73% of Yemenis, with large differences between different European countries, owing to the different diplomatic stances among EU Member States.

In 2015, according to UNHCR, Greece received the largest share of newcomers, who then tried to enter other EU Member States. The EU-Turkish agreements of March 2016 stopped most sea crossings between Greece and Turkey. However, many asylum seekers were held in camps, such as that on the island of Lesbos, for months or even years, without any resolution to their request for refugee status, in physical conditions that contravened their human rights (Le Blanc & Brugère, 2017). The "soft diplomacy" involved in this case had several dimensions: following the agreement with Turkey, Greece was grateful to Angela Merkel for her role in creating this arrangement, which came after years of conflict between Greece and the EU (and particularly Germany) owing to Greece's debt situation. On this matter the German chancellor thus won some recognition from Greece.

3.2 II – The Refugee Crisis of 2015: Path Dependency, Crises of Solidarity, and Unanimity Rule in Brussels

The main reasons for the failure of managing the reception of refugees in Europe are to be found in European immigration and asylum policy itself. Since 1990, most instruments of dissuasion, repression, and confinement have involved European immigration and asylum policy. The Frontex mechanism for policing Europe's external borders (created in 2004 as a joint European police force at the external borders of the EU, and implemented from 2005) had its funding renewed and increased several times over (Rodier, 2019). The principles of the Dublin agreements on asylum were not questioned.

The greatest failure was the crisis of solidarity between EU Member States. In previous years, the approach most commonly proposed by large countries of destination for refugees was that of sharing the burden, which was notably adopted by Germany and Austria after the fall of the Berlin Wall. However, the Dublin II regime effectively transferred the task of receiving refugees to Southern EU Member States with a Mediterranean coast, particularly Italy and Greece. A second crisis of solidarity appeared in 2015 between Eastern and Western EU Member States with regard to EU proposals for the resettlement of refugees: most countries belonging to the Visegrad group (Poland, Hungary, the Czech Republic, and Slovakia) refused to receive newcomers and closed their national borders. Solidarity, one of the values of the EU, as defined in the EU Treaty of Lisbon (2007), collapsed owing to a lack of trust between EU Member States regarding the management of refugees, and also as a result of the growing strength of nationalist ideologies all over Europe. These Eastern European countries were not ostracised for their positions: no judgements were passed (although trials were conducted in the cases of Poland, the Czech Republic, and Hungary), no fines were imposed (a fine of €250,000 for each asylum seeker rejected was proposed but never implemented), and these states did not face any cuts to the structural EU funds that they were receiving. The refugee crisis gave rise to many such cases of the return of national borders and assertions of national sovereignty, such as at the border between France and Italy (2011 and 2015), between Hungary and its neighbours (2015), and between Bulgaria and Greece (2016).

The weakness of the EU on these matters is partly due to the requirement for a unanimous vote to pass any measures on migration and asylum affairs at the European Council. This system gives individual countries considerable power to veto any possibility of reforming the Dublin agreements, even though these are strongly criticised by all NGOs and associations involved in taking care of newcomers. Other approaches on the part of the EU would be possible but have not even been debated, such as implementing a 2001 European directive on providing temporary protection for newcomers who do not fit the criteria of the Geneva Convention definition of refugees, or creating an obligation to receive boats of refugees crossing the Mediterranean, thus saving people at risk of dying at sea. It would also be possible to reopen legal channels for labour immigration, which would reduce the proliferation of so-called mixed flows of job seekers attempting to get refugee status. The weakness of Euro-Mediterranean dialogue and the adherence to old failed solutions, such as return policies (as decided at the Valletta Euro-African summit of autumn 2015 and again in 2019) are also part of the crisis, which is ultimately more a crisis of solidarity than of refugees themselves.

An externalisation of borders beyond the EU space led EU Member States to sign bilateral and multilateral agreements with many extra-European neighbours asking them to control their borders with Europe in exchange for money, visas for their elites, and development aid, even in non-safe countries.

A renewal of the migration crisis occurred in 2020 when President Erdoğan began to reopen the borders of Turkey to refugees wishing to enter Europe to apply for a refugee status that they could not get in Turkey. Turkey signed the Geneva Convention of 1951, but never extended its definition of refugees to include non-Europeans (whereas the New York Protocol on Refugees of 1967 extended access to refugee status to the whole world). In a game of soft diplomacy with Europe, Turkey threatened Europe with the arrival of thousands of newcomers on Greek shores, where the situation was critical owing to the COVID-19 crisis. Instead of proposing to share the burden of newcomers among the 27 EU Member States, the EU opted to help Greece, at a time when public opinion was protesting day after day against the existence of refugee camps. Turkey's use of asylum as a bargaining chip to obtain concessions that it had not received in 2016 brings to mind the opposition between Belarus and Poland in autumn 2021, when Belarus organised the arrival of Middle Eastern refugee flows at the Polish border (and thus an external EU border) in order to apply pressure and reinforce its demands upon the EU.

Faced with these migration crises, which challenge policymakers and are a subject of intense political controversies, European leaders are trying to find ways to cope with one of the largest refugee flows in European history without contradicting public opinion, which is increasingly influenced by populist parties. However, attempts to "manage" the situation through security-orientated and anti-immigration policy instruments, both by individual Member States and collective EU measures, seem to provide limited results. Meanwhile, these measures have serious adverse effects: thousands of deaths in the Mediterranean Sea, the emergence of both formal and informal camps for detaining migrants, increasing tensions on the borders of Europe, the violation of rights and legal provisions at the national, European, and international level, and the proliferation of human smuggling, trafficking, and other criminal activities around migration and migrants.

Why do policy makers adhere to decisions and policy options that seem to have failed to achieve their explicit goals in the past? The refugee crisis has revealed the social mechanisms underpinning this process (organisations, human smuggling, which is becoming a pull factor, and push factors linked to political crises and unemployment), the different and conflicting ways in which EU Member States and EU institutions have responded to the influx of migrants, the lack of trust between Northern and Southern European Member States amid the refugee crisis of 2015, and the ongoing inability of Europe to find a solution to the treatment of refugees.

3.2.1 The Ukrainian Case: An Exception?

The invasion of Ukraine by Russia in February 2022 brought about a new approach to the crisis of hospitality and solidarity towards refugees in Europe. The same countries that had previously been particularly reluctant to receive newcomers were very willing to receive their neighbours from Ukraine as refugees. Through a multilevel reception policy, which was decided at the EU level with the implementation of temporary protection measures according to a directive of 2001 (first formulated for Kosovars and never applied before 2022), Ukrainians were received in Europe and institutionally settled thanks to public policies at national and local level. These settlement programmes involved housing refugees in the homes of citizens, which was a method implemented in Germany in 2015. Poland, Hungary, the Czech Republic, Romania, and Moldova were the countries most heavily involved in the reception of refugees, for historical reasons (the movement of borders since the end of the Second Wold War) and owing to the shared memory of facing a Russian enemy (Budapest in 1956, Prague in 1968, the Solidarność movement in 1980). Ukrainians, being white, Christian Europeans, were more readily accepted in those countries, and also in Western Europe, owing to the selective approach used to distinguish between European and non-European refugees.

3.3 Conclusion: Is There a Migration Diplomacy Around Refugee Policies?

After a period of 30 years in which research on refugees in political science and international relations was rare (because the topic was mostly treated in the field of international law), there has more recently been a large number of publications. We would point first of all to the works of Aristide Zolberg (Zolberg et al., 1989), Emma Haddad (2008), and Karen Akoka (2020). Aristide Zolberg particularly emphasises the place of the Global South in the refugee question. Emma Haddad, like Zolberg, analyses refugees as actors in the relationship between the internal political order and international affairs. She considers that the arrival of refugees on the international scene gives rise to a mismatch between the theory and practice of the international system and the concept of the sovereignty of states: whereas the concept of the migrant belongs to the national order of states, the concept of the refugee is a political construct which transcends the state-citizen-territory model. Refugees, as international actors, exist only in a context of international societies of sovereign states with borders between them. They therefore challenge the classical international order of states, and they are now becoming central actors on the international scene. Whereas the migrant is heavily dependent on the practices of individual nation states, refugees do not belong to states as such, thus escaping from the logics of states, nationalities, and territories, as they are protected by an international status recognised by the United Nations.

In her book on asylum and exile (2020), Karen Akoka argues that the bottom-up treatment of refugees reveals a parallel system of diplomacy. Two main historical trends can be seen in the treatment of refugees: during the Cold War, the reception of refugees was linked with foreign policy, and both in the East and the West refugees were admitted based on their nationality alone, with acceptance rates of 99% for Vietnamese or Chilean asylum seekers; in recent decades, the reception of refugees has become a matter of domestic border control, with rates of acceptance decreasing to levels between 50% and 70%. However, some exceptions can be observed: in the French case, in the 1960s and 1970s, Portuguese, Spanish, and Yugoslavs were barely recognised as statutory refugees because public policy was aimed at preserving good relations with these regimes. Since these nationalities were in demand as a source of labour, when these migrants arrived without documentation they were legalised as workers. Until 1965, most refugees were perceived as being orphaned from their former national status (mostly in cases of states that had ceased to exist) rather than as persecuted victims. There was a collective recognition for all refugees coming from behind the Iron Curtain and for Vietnamese. The turning point of the 1990s is linked to a subordination of asylum issues to security-based policies for border control, leading to rates of recognition below 20% in 1990–2000 for Sub-Saharan Africans. However, the profiles of these migrants were individually filtered, owing to the will to preserve good relations with some African presidents, as well as a fear in public opinion of an African "invasion". The present discourse on mixed flows, which blurs distinctions between asylum seekers and job seekers, is rooted in this practice, without acknowledging it.

References

Akoka, K. (2020). *L'asile et l'exil*. La découverte.
Haddad, E. (2008). *The refugee in international society: Between sovereigns*. Cambridge University Press.
Le Blanc, G., & Brugère, F. (2017). *La fin de l'hospitalité: Lampedusa, Lesbos, Calais*. Flammarion.
Rodier, C. (2019). L'équation lucrative du contrôle des frontières. *L'Economie Politique: Alternatives Économiques, 84*. https://www.alternatives-economiques.fr/lequation-lucrative-controle-frontieres/00090972
UNHCR. (2022). *The state of the World refugees*.
Zolberg, A., Suhrke, A., & Aguayo, S. (1989). *Escape from violence: Conflict and the refugee crisis in the developing world*. Oxford University Press.

Open Access This chapter is licensed under the terms of the Creative Commons Attribution 4.0 International License (http://creativecommons.org/licenses/by/4.0/), which permits use, sharing, adaptation, distribution and reproduction in any medium or format, as long as you give appropriate credit to the original author(s) and the source, provide a link to the Creative Commons license and indicate if changes were made.

The images or other third party material in this chapter are included in the chapter's Creative Commons license, unless indicated otherwise in a credit line to the material. If material is not included in the chapter's Creative Commons license and your intended use is not permitted by statutory regulation or exceeds the permitted use, you will need to obtain permission directly from the copyright holder.

Chapter 4
Citizenship and Migration in the International Order

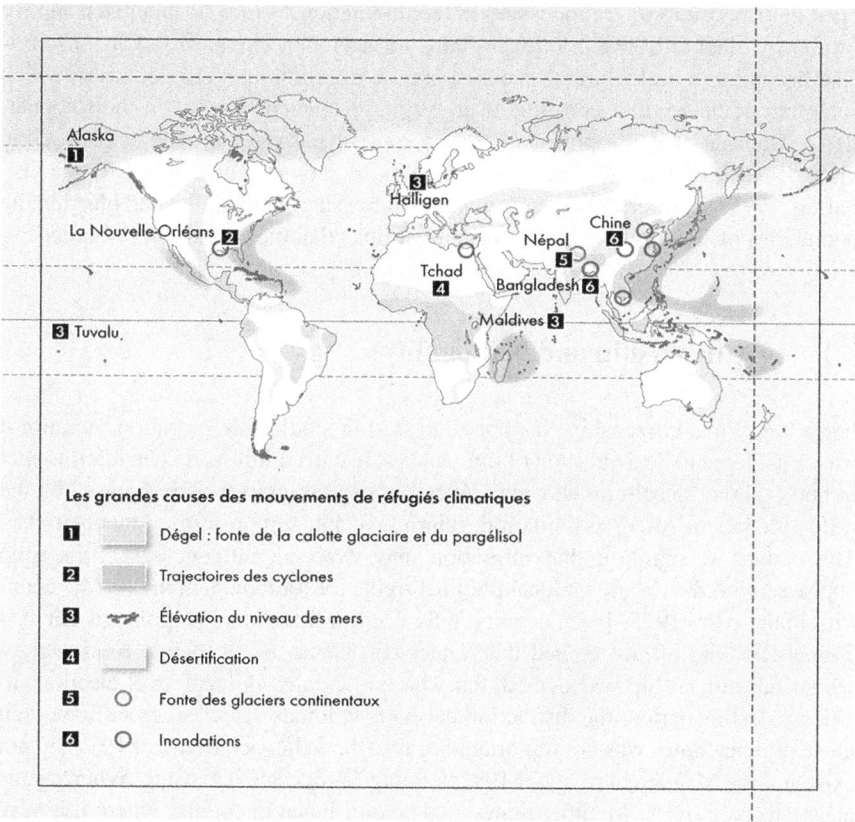

The factors of environmentally displaced migrations
Alaska, New Orleans, Tuvalu, Halligen, Chad, Maldivian Islands, Bangladesh, Nepal, China
Legend: Main causes of movements of climate refugees

1. Thaw of water from Arctic areas
2. Storms trajectories
3. Rise of sea levels
4. Desertification of soils
5. Smelting of continental ices
6. Floods

© The Author(s) 2023
C. Wihtol de Wenden, *Migration and International Relations*, IMISCOE
Research Series, https://doi.org/10.1007/978-3-031-31716-3_4

Citizenship is usually defined in terms of the rights and duties of citizens in relation to nation states. The definition used in France refers to the philosophical content of the social contract and the values of the Declaration of the Rights of Man and of the Citizen of 1789, whereas in most countries it refers to nationality rights (which are specifically conceived in terms of "nationality" in France). However, the concept of citizenship is now being challenged by migration, because the nation state is no longer the only reference in terms of individuals' belonging. Transnational diasporas, border-crossing experiences, and the existence of large numbers of undocumented migrants are calling into question both the international system of national borders and the concept of citizenship, since various forms of citizenship have developed in response to migration issues in the international order (local citizenship for foreigners, dual citizenship, refugee status for asylum seekers, etc.). Citizenship is also becoming a multicultural phenomenon in large immigration countries, which sometimes change their constitution in response to such changes in their populations. Transnational diasporas, as new actors in the international order (acting through "the strength of weak ties", as Mark Granovetter puts it; 1973; see also Safran, 1991; Scheffer, 2006) are becoming increasingly influential and blurring the boundaries of states owing to the diversity of links that they build across borders.

4.1 I – Citizenship and Nationality

For a long time, citizenship was not addressed in studies on migration, because it was considered to be a question of internal law, usually addressed as an afterthought in books about constitutional rights. Approaches to migration were focused on the needs for labour force, assimilation, return, and integration in the labour market. The earliest recognition that migration may exert an influence on citizenship appeared with the debate on local political rights for foreigners in the Nordic countries in the years 1975–1985, notably in Sweden. A little later, the political scientist Tomas Hammar (1990) coined the concept of "denizens" to define foreigners to whom full citizenship was denied, but who participated in local level elections as citizens. In this period, the distinction between nationals of EU Member States and those of other states was not important because the Schengen treaty of 1985 did not exist, nor the Maastricht treaty of 1992 defining European Citizenship. Whereas this question arose in EU Member States, and also in Japan (a country where it is very difficult for foreigners to acquire citizenship), it did not arise in countries of immigration of settlement that apply the principle of *jus soli*, such as the US, Canada, and Australia. In these countries, citizenship is acquired at birth and naturalisation is rapidly granted to new settlers.

A new approach to citizenship also emerged in the years 1990–1995, in connection with the concept of transnationalism. Transnational citizenship is a particularly relevant approach in contexts of migration, since migrants build links across borders through their diasporas. The geographical extent of citizenship thus becomes more important than its limitation to the borders of the nation state, as conceived in its traditional definition. Authors such as Rainer Bauböck (1994) and Yasemin Soysal

(1994) developed this concept further in a period when transnationalism was rapidly increasing in the world owing to the growth in cross-border mobility following the fall of the Iron Curtain. Meanwhile, older waves of migration continued to reinforce transborder links through associative and cultural networks, marriage practices, transnational trade, and entrepreneurship across borders.

The growth in multiculturalism also had an influence on citizenship in the 1990–2000s. This issue was raised by authors such as Will Kymlicka (1995) in Canada, Stephen Castles in Australia, and John Rex and Guharpal Singh in the UK (2004). Multiculturalism leads to an enlargement of the concept of citizenship, with the addition of values of diversity and ethics of anti-discrimination. The concept was also developed in Germany and in the Netherlands, but was later abandoned and replaced with more integrationist approaches. Angela Merkel herself publicly declared that multiculturalism in Germany had failed.

4.1.1 *The French Case: Distinction Between Citizenship and Nationality*

In France, citizenship is linked to secularism ("laïcité"), a concept that was defined by the law of 1905 concerning the separation of church and state, and which returned to prominence in the 1990s in relation to the place of Islam in public life (controversy around the wearing of Muslim types of headscarf in 1989, and more generally the visibility of Islam in public space, such as prayer rooms, halal butchers, Muslim libraries, and other manifestations of Islamic ways of life). Those who attempted to find a new form of citizenship of immigrant origin, while remaining Muslim, found themselves involved in many different negotiations, as documented in various field studies (Kepel, 1987; Etienne, 1989; Cesari, 1994; Leveau & Mohsen, 2005).

While many immigration countries use only one word in this context (so that there is no distinction between citizenship and nationality), in France the two words are used differently: citizenship refers to the rights and duties of a citizen, while nationality refers to the legal distinction between French people and foreigners. More than a century ago, France became the first country to make a change in the law governing access to nationality from *jus sanguinis* (introduced by Napoleon I in the Civil Code of 1804, and also applied in conquered lands) to one based on a balance between *jus sanguinis* and *jus soli*. This change was intended to make it easier to incorporate foreigners into the nation state. However, despite its long history of immigration, France never considered immigration as part of its founding national myth. Its republican model was built on shared political consensus around the values of the French Revolution (freedom, equality, and fraternity), without any reference to ethnic or regional origins. Yet, in periods of low demographic growth during the nineteenth and early twentieth century, there was a need to grant access to French nationality to newcomers in order to meet the need for soldiers and future citizens. The law of 1889 extended access for foreigners to French nationality, through an extension of *jus soli* to apply to those born in France or having been resident in France (Weil, 2004). New debates instigated by the far right in France on possible reforms to the laws governing nationality, and a possible change in the application of the principles of *jus soli* and *jus sanguinis*, have often made reference to dark periods of France's history from the 1940s (for example, the possibility of "déchéance de nationalité" – the withdrawal of nationality from someone who had previously acquired it). Nonetheless, after fierce debates between 1988 and 1998, France continues to apply policies involving a balance between *jus soli and jus sanguinis*. Most EU Member States, having formerly managed access to nationality by *jus sanguinis* (except for the UK) reformed their laws in this domain in the years 1990–2000. For example, a century after France, Germany introduced a principle of *jus soli* into its citizenship laws in order to incorporate foreigners who had previously had only limited possibilities for acquiring German citizenship. Italy continues to apply *jus sanguinis*, as defined by a law of 1913.

In parallel, multiculturalism has also challenged the French model of citizenship, which is strongly linked with the nation state, owing to the pressure of migration within the EU and that of second generation immigrants who had become nationals. Whereas in the 1960s the term "assimilation" was still used in public discourse (since the 1880s), the term "integration" began to be used at the end of the Algerian War of Indepedence, and was adopted in 1974 by the Secretary of State for Immigration Paul Dijoud. The aim was to abandon the individualist and authoritarian approach associated with "assimilation" in favour of an expression of cultural diversity, in order to help foreigners to feel that they belonged. The particular situation of Islam in France gave some specificity to the French approach to integration: the headscarf affair of 1989 and then the law of 2004 prohibiting the wearing of visible religious signs in schools brought an emphasis on secularism as a republican value to be shared by future citizens, while the value of "fraternity" was seriously challenged by the recognition of a "social gap" (Jacques Chirac described this gap as a "fracture sociale" during his presidential campaign in 1995).

Despite being an old country of immigration, France developed a political myth based on philosophical values (the "social contract") in order to bring more homogeneity to a diverse population made up of many cultures in its various "provinces", with their own languages and specific ways of life. In spite of its republican myth, France is a multicultural country. This blindness towards immigration and internal diversity is connected with France's founding national myth, which is mostly built on the heritage of the Revolution. When the Third Republic, established in 1875, announced its ambition to create a system of free, compulsory, secular primary education (through the laws of 1882 and 1884), in which 80% of the pupils would be the children of peasants, it created a need to formulate a shared history, acceptable to all, and which would contribute to the creation of educated republican citizens. It was a particular priority to write a consensual history of France. Ernest Lavisse (2014), Professor at the prestigious Collège de France, was appointed to this task. He created the citizen-myth of the "Gaulois", centred on the image of an autochthonous French population invaded by foreigners (the Romans, the "Francs", the Arabs). Thus, in spite of the considerable cultural and ethnic diversity of France, represented by its division into the countries of the "langue d'Oïl" in the North and of the "langue d'Oc "in the South, it became a unified country by means of centralised rules that made no reference to ethnic belonging or foreign components. This myth of autochthony progressively came to characterise representations of the country, in opposition to various forms of cosmopolitanism. It is now a major source of inspiration for populist political parties (this conception of France is particularly used by the populist right wing politicians Marine Le Pen and Éric Zemmour; Wihtol de Wenden, 2004).

4.2 II – Citizenship and Migration in a Globalised World

Globalisation, as one of the main factors affecting mobility, also has an impact on the nature of citizenship, which was formerly mainly determined by nation states. The new gap that has emerged between a universal right to emigrate and a discretionary right to immigrate is creating a new disorder. Global inequality in terms of the right to mobility, depending on an individual's nationality and passport, is leading to the emergence of various forms of citizenship, mostly as a result of localised negotiations, involving many possibilities for agency but also many exclusions (Wihtol de Wenden, 2013).

Many forms of transnational citizenship have appeared, with many forms of double presence, both at the national and international level. The concept of transnational citizenship also changes the definition of belonging. The hierarchy of citizenship is also challenged when new nationals go on to be considered as "others", with a major segmentation between different statuses of nationals, just as can be observed in the case of citizenship in Europe. Indeed, we can observe a hierarchy with, at the top, nationals living in their country of origin, followed by nationals of other EU Member States, then long-term extra-European residents and statutory refugees, then short-term extra-European migrants, then asylum seekers and irregular migrants. More broadly, mobility weakens the relationship between the citizen and the state (Wihtol de Wenden, 2017).

The globalisation of migration has led to an evolution in the concept of citizenship. Citizenship was formerly confined to the nation state, linking the citizen to exclusive rights and duties towards the state of belonging. With increasing mobility, as well as multiple affiliations for those who are settled, new forms of citizenship continue to appear. These new forms of citizenship include multiple allegiances and policies in countries of both destination and departure that create links with their members. Meanwhile, debates and policies related to integration lead second generation migrants to rebuild their identities as citizens and nationals, while newcomers may be totally excluded (Leveau & Wihtol de Wenden, 2001).

4.2.1 Citizenship Challenged by Migration

Migration brings new challenges to established models of citizenship, owing to the increasing diversification and globalisation of migration, the new forms of dissociation that it creates between nationality and citizenship, and the emergence of transnational forms of citizenship that cross borders and mix identities.

4.2.1.1 Citizenship in a World of Mobility

Do migrants have access to a legitimate form of citizenship in a world on the move, where mobility is considered as an element of modernity and a factor of human development, but where those who remain in place have more rights than those who are mobile? The question is particularly pressing in the case of international migration, since many categories of migrants do not attain a legal existence in this mobile world. Some people wish to define mobility as a world public good (this is the aim of the GFMD, as announced by Kofi Annan in 2006; Badie et al., 2008), a new human right for the twenty-first century, while others consider that mobility is introducing disorder into the world of nation states.

Some countries, such as Canada and Australia, have built their history on migration and adapted their particular concept of citizenship in relation to newcomers, so as to build an identity based on migration and diversity. Many migrants do not have any citizenship status in the countries where they live. This includes undocumented people, refused asylum seekers, stateless people, and environmentally displaced persons. All of these categories of migrants disturb the order of nation states, whether as refugees, foreigners, Europeans, or double nationals; they transgress the link between nationals and their state, they do not belong to the nation state territory where they reside, they do not necessarily speak the national language (or languages), and they may not be involved in all the laws of the country. Conversely, the nation state loses its control over a part of its population, its borders, and more broadly over the population-state-territory nexus.

In matters of migration, citizenship cannot be considered in its traditional context (Castles & Davidson, 2000; Castles, 1997). Most previous research on migration and citizenship viewed the migrant as a future citizen in the country of destination, or as an actor in relation to the country of origin. Most migrants in Northern Europe effectively became second class citizens, or "denizens" (Hammar, 1990), even when they acquired local political rights without full citizenship. With globalisation, we are faced with segmented forms of citizenship, mostly belonging to a hierarchy, despite the fact that citizenship has been extended at the local level in some cases, and the fact that dual citizens can benefit from citizenship both in their countries of origin and of destination. Second generation migrants have also contributed to the emergence of new concepts of belonging, with multiple allegiances and transnational forms of citizenship, thanks to the international networks formed by diasporas. For many migrants, the "double absence" that was formerly experienced by migrant workers (Sayad, 1999), as a foreigner in both the country of origin and the country of destination, has now been transformed into a double presence, and they have been able to adopt mobility as a way of life, benefitting from systems of visas and free circulation. These new migrant citizens offer an example of citizenship based mainly on residence and participation, thereby dissociating citizenship from migration and introducing new values into the classical model of citizenship, such as those of anti-discrimination and diversity.

While the norm of the national order is the citizen living in the state in which they have citizenship and are resident, subject to the rights and duties defined by that state, the rules of belonging and allegiance are different for mobile populations, for whom the nation state is not significant (rejected asylum seekers, the stateless, irregular migrants, etc.). In other cases, allegiances and belonging have no meaning in countries where one can buy a passport or become a legal resident if one brings enough money, buys enough real estate property, or creates a company.

4.2.1.2 Dissociation Between Nationality and Citizenship

This dissociation between nationality and citizenship, created by the development of EU citizenship, but also by EU Member States that decided to grant local citizenship to foreigners, is one of the most important consequences of changes to models of citizenship in Europe (Wihtol de Wenden, 1997). Since 1975, systems for granting local political rights to all foreigners in Northern European countries (Sweden in 1975, Denmark in 1981, the Netherlands in 1985, Belgium in 2000, Switzerland in some places, such as Neuchâtel and Jura, and the UK for Commonwealth citizens) introduced the possibility of a dissociation between nationality and citizenship. 15 EU Member States out of 27 have granted local citizenship to extra-European nationals.

Meanwhile, all EU citizens living in an EU Member State other than their country of origin can be local citizens in that new country without being a national, if they participate as voters or as elected local representatives in political life. Conversely, in the past there were nationals who were not citizens, in the cases of criminal punishments, colonial indigenous statuses, reduced rights for women and the disabled, and military corps in France during the Third Republic.

These new forms of citizenship without nationality place emphasis on residence, local roots, participation in local politics, and multiple belongings. They are more inclusive, more detached from nationality rights and territories, and they further extend the limits of citizenship to include transnational links and networks between migrants, their countries of origin (if they continue to enjoy from national and local voting rights there), and their diasporas. They may give migrants greater influence both in their countries of origin and in receiving countries.

4.2.1.3 *Extension of* Jus Soli

Most EU Nation States (with the exception of Italy) have also granted access to citizenship for newcomers by adopting the principle of *jus soli*, rather than exclusively applying the principle of *jus sanguinis*, in order to be more inclusive to newcomers and their children born in the country of immigration. Rogers Brubaker (2000) has shown that rights of access to nationality and naturalisation policies have an impact on political integration for newcomers. There is, however, no compensation or reciprocity between countries that grant more access to citizenship rights and those that grant more access to local political rights: some countries that are reluctant to grant local citizenship also restrict access to nationality, while others grant easier access both to nationality and to local citizenship rights. Japan, while intending to grant some local political rights to foreigners, in fact makes it very difficult to access Japanese citizenship. Until 2000, Germany was reluctant both to develop local political rights for foreigners and to open nationality to residence criteria. On the contrary, New Zealand grants local political rights and is a country of *jus soli*.

4.2.1.4 Transnational Citizenship

Transnational migration has led to forms of transnational citizenship, with multiple allegiances and diasporic networks, giving rise to new forms of political influence and intrusion. This is sometimes used as a form of migration diplomacy by countries of origin that become diasporic states, such as the diplomacy conducted in Europe by Turkey or Morocco, whose migrants are spread across various EU Member States and develop networks through migration links. This transnational citizenship, studied by Rainer Bauböck (1994) and Yasemin Soysal (1994), shows the extent to which citizenship can be experienced and activated through migration. This expression of citizenship beyond borders enlarges the limits of the nation state, as an alternative to classical definitions of citizenship.

Transnationalism leads to a questioning of the dynamics of states, networks, and non-state actors. According to Bauböck (1994), citizenship is based on consensual belonging and free entry into transnational citizenship, owing either to escape or adhesion (according to Hirschman's model; 1970). The right to mobility contradicts the link between the citizen and the state. In most examples, multiculturalism emerged from the failure of bi-national states (in the case of Canada) or the impossible dream of a homogeneous state (in the case of Australia). In many nation states, multiculturalism conflicts with a myth of national homogeneity, which derives from a constructivist approach developed in the late nineteenth century. In particular, the myth of autochthony is often so strong (such as in France, but also in Central and Eastern Europe) that it creates artificial internal borders built on ethnicity or religion, and suspects the "other" of maintaining dubious allegiances in contexts of international conflict (such as during the Dreyfus affair in 1898 in France). All immigration countries have some concerns about the assimilation or integration of foreigners, and multiculturalism was proposed as a model of citizenship and national identity. Multicultural citizenship has acquired some legitimacy in Europe (the value of "diversity" was inscribed in the Lisbon Treaty of 2007), Australia, Canada, and the US, and it may foster universal values such as anti-discrimination, cultural pluralism, dialogue between religions, hospitality, and living together. However, it continues to be strongly challenged by populist and far right political parties on the grounds of their concerns about national identities.

4.2.2 The Multiple Forms of Negotiated Citizenship

In the mid-twentieth century, the negotiation of new forms of citizenship acquired some legitimacy in countries that had already begun to define themselves as countries of immigration, such as Canada and Australia. In this process, an important role was played by transnational mobilisations that had been developed by migrants struggling to attain the desired legal status, as well as by associations and NGOs advocating for greater rights for migrants.

4.2.2.1 Dual Citizenship: An Individual Solution for Mobile Citizens

With globalised mobility, migrants are becoming actors in a multidimensional space. Experiencing mobility as a "double presence" requires access to dual citizenship, although this is prohibited by certain countries of origin. Many emigration countries, such as Turkey and countries of the Maghreb, were formerly opposed to dual citizenship but have now made this available to their departing nationals. Dual citizenship is now easier to obtain owing to the continuing application of *jus sanguinis* in Islamic emigration countries and to the extension of *jus soli* in immigration countries. In the past, former migrants were viewed as undeserving subjects or illegitimate citizens in their countries of origin when they acquired nationality in immigration countries. The acceptance of dual nationality by many emigration countries developed in the 1990s, when they started to understand the benefit that this could bring in terms of using their dual citizens to exert international influence on immigration countries (through the power of dual citizens as a voting bloc, as well as through networks of elites and diasporic associations). In the past, migrants who became nationals in immigration countries viewed their nationality in the country of origin as becoming dormant. Whereas, in the Cold War era, refugees obtained nationality in their countries of destination without maintaining any hope of returning to their country of origin, it later became possible for some refugees to return to their country of origin when, for example, a certain conflict had ended (this corresponds to the "cessation clause" defined in the Geneva Convention of 1951).

The concept of membership lies at the centre of the concept of dual citizenship. For the second generation, mobility becomes easier, more affordable (with the exception of some visas), and can be conducted through legal channels. While most of these new citizens simply consider themselves as citizens, they may also be viewed as a security threat in the context of Islamic attacks. When they act as professional soldiers in the army of their immigration country, they serve without any feeling of divided loyalty (Bertossi & Wihtol de Wenden, 2007) in conflicts in Islamic countries (Afghanistan, Iraq), but they are sometimes viewed with suspicion. For these migrants, dual citizenship is also a solution to the problem that the passport of their former country provided limited opportunities for mobility compared with "good" passports (European, American, Canadian, etc.).

4.2.2.2 Refugees

The other main type of agency developed by migrants is that of seeking refugee rights. The crisis of 2015 showed the importance of political asylum for those fleeing wars and conflicts, especially since access to EU Member States is very limited for those looking for work. Seeking asylum is therefore a form of agency leading to a legal status, in cases where the receiving state accepts the asylum seeker's narrative of persecution. Many migration flows now appear to be mixed flows, since seeking asylum provides the only possibility to enter legally with no documents, in cases of emergency, and in the absence of possibilities for economic migration. For asylum applicants, choosing this route may lead to a restrictive access to refugee status and a politicisation of their profiles. In 2015, half of asylum seekers were accepted as refugees in Germany and 40% in France. In earlier decades (1980–2000), the refusal of refugee status was the norm, and acceptance was the exception. Compared with the Cold War period, when the rate of acceptance was very high because individuals were mostly considered as being victims of the communist world, newcomers since the 1990s have had less individualised profiles, but rather belonged to specific collective groups that have been persecuted by their state of origin or by civil society, owing to their ethnic, religious, or sexual characteristics, or their social categories. The refugee profile transcends the conceptual nexus of state-citizen-territory. As an international actor, the refugee is viewed as bringing disorder to the international order of nation states, while benefitting from a universal status. Other protections (provisional and humanitarian) are the result of negotiated agencies between states and NGOs. Sub-Saharan applicants generally have greater difficultly in being recognised as refugees, since they are widely viewed as false refugees by most nation states.

4.2.2.3 Environmentally Displaced Persons

Another form of agency is the international mobilisation to institute an official status for environmentally displaced persons. The term "environmentally displaced person" or "climate refugee" appeared at the end of the 1980s, mainly connected to climate change, although there are many other forms of environmental threat that can give rise to refugees. However, none of these conditions have been recognised with an international status. According to the IPCC (Intergovernmental Panel on Climate Change), there could be as many as 150 or 200 million environmentally displaced persons by the end of this century, but attempts to grant them an official status have failed because the UNHCR does not consider them as escaping from persecution. There is, however, some agency in this matter on the part of NGOs, although the migrants concerned are among the poorest in the world, and are widely dispersed all around the world. Bangladesh is one of the foremost countries to be threatened by large flows of environmentally displaced persons, and it has tried to direct its diplomacy in UN circles towards this issue. The variety of types of environmental threats also makes it difficult to develop an argument at the international level, although the question is far from being new (threats such as earthquakes, droughts, volcanic eruptions, and floods have always been a part of human history). Environmentally displaced persons usually seek protection at the regional level, and most look for shelter in their own country, so as to continue or regain their usual way of life. In all cases, the law has been unable to offer a solution to these new forms of forced mobility, since debate continues to be stalled by the question of the nature of these threats as "persecution", and that of whether this migration is voluntary or forced.

4.2.2.4 Statelessness

Statelessness became a major problem at the international level after the First World War as a result of the collapse of several of the former Great Empires (the Ottoman Empire, the Russian Empire, the Austro-Hungarian Empire) and the expulsion of some minorities from new nation states. There are currently around 13 million stateless people living in the world, despite a UN international agreement of 1954 that aimed to reduce cases of statelessness. For example, the Rohingya in Bangladesh do not have any legal acceptance in this country, nor in Myanmar, where they come from. There are also stateless people in Africa (particularly the Great Lakes region) and in Europe (residents of the Helligen islands between Germany, Denmark, and the Baltic states, who were not granted European citizenship owing to their belonging to the Russian community and their inability to speak national Baltic languages – thus holding so-called "grey" passports). Most stateless people are refugees, but not all, since in some cases they have lived in the same place for a long time, and they have been made stateless by historic developments. Whereas a refugee has citizenship in their country of origin, a stateless person does not have any citizenship, and therefore lacks any diplomatic protection. Some stateless people are also victims of denationalisation procedures (when they have lost their nationality of the country of origin). There are global efforts to reduce the number of stateless people, but many states have no interest in this question.

4.2.2.5 Denizens

The term "denizens" was adopted by Tomas Hammar to describe foreigners (European or extra-European) who were denied full citizenship when they were granted local citizenship rights in the mid-1970s by Sweden. Many other EU Member States granted local citizenship to foreigners during the 1980s and 1990s. In 1992 the Maastricht Treaty extended these local rights to all EU citizens living in another EU Nation State, thus making non-nationals into citizens at the local level. However, for non-Europeans, the principle of "citizenship of residence" was gradually used to seek voting rights, as associations advocating for the defence of voting rights pointed out that those (non-Europeans) who had been settled for a long time were not allowed to vote at the local level, whereas short-term settled EU citizens were eligible to vote after only a short presence (Wihtol de Wenden, 1997). Many national constitutions were altered in order to introduce European and non-European citizenship into their rules relating to democracy and sovereignty.

4.2.2.6 Irregular Migrants, or "Illegals"

The last category includes all those who are refused any status of protection or link with the migration state: this includes refused asylum seekers, ill people without any protection, and people who were formerly unaccompanied minors but then reach the age of adulthood. There is a high degree of activism among these migrants and the human rights associations that support them, generally aimed at legalising irregular migrants or granting refugee status.

The role of political agency has been crucial during the last 30 years on several different fronts: defining a concept of citizenship dissociated from nationality, introducing the cultural values of diversity, cosmopolitanism and anti-discrimination, promoting a model of "good citizenship" through the acceptance of dual citizenship, naturalisation, and the legalisation of the undocumented, and struggling to make refugee status more accessible. In receiving countries, civil society has played an important role in defending access to rights, but this has always been a work in progress. In countries of origin, the emergence of forms of migration diplomacy in international forums has also led to greater inclusion for migrants.

The presence of "illegals" underscores the failure of states to control their borders at the global scale, and the lack of international governance on this issue. Human rights associations draw attention to the daily life of the so-called undocumented in camps, "jungles", and other contexts of abject living conditions and social exclusion.

4.2.2.7 Citizens But Not True Citizens: Discrimination and Autochthony

What Michel Wieviorka defines as "differentialist racism", and which other sociologists name "institutional racism from institutions of authority", relates to discrimination based on denying citizenship to some citizens because they are considered as being illegitimate. In France, as in many immigration countries, some white, generally poor citizens claim that they are "true citizens", owing to their roots in that country (in France, the term "Français de souche" is used in this context) (Wieviorka, 1994), in comparison with other citizens whom they consider as being "less French", because they are visibly racialized, Muslim (although France is a secular country), and belong to a distinct group. The manifestations of institutional racism appear frequently: police discrimination leading to police violence committed by police officers towards visibly racialized people (especially young people walking in groups in inner city areas), discriminatory use of stop-and-search powers, systemic racist discourse related to the Algerian War, and confusion between individuals and the ethnic groups to which they are assumed to belong. Generalised fears become legitimised by instances of terrorism, urban riots, and problems within communities. A certain proportion of the population does not see the nation in terms of social and political cohesion, but in terms of a division between those who are truly French and those who are not. In the public sphere, there has long been a tolerance towards institutional racism committed by the police and the army. The UK and the US began to try to address problems of institutional discrimination earlier than in France, but it remains a problem in both cases (as highlighted by the case of the murder of George Floyd by a police officer, and the social divisions that it exacerbated) (Body-Gendrot & Wihtol de Wenden, 2014). Most immigration countries use ethnic statistics as a tool against these kinds of discrimination. In France, an increasing number of voices are arguing that this practice could help to fight against systemic discrimination. However, the Constitutional Council rejected this proposal in 2007, arguing that it would be contrary to the image of France as indivisible, and would therefore legitimate ethnic determinisms in a country which has never defined itself in terms of ethnic belonging. Since 2000, EU directives have prohibited discrimination, mainly at work, but street and institutional racism are still far from being recognised and punished.

4.3 Conclusion

The contradictions inherent in a world in which everything is free to circulate except humans have been analysed by Sigmunt Bauman, who refers to Kant's definition of universal citizenship, while distinguishing between the right to visit and the right to settlement (Bauman, 2000). Citizenship becomes a problematic concept in a world characterised by mobility, since the classical definition of citizenship does not easily fit with this global context. Thanks to migration, debates on the various forms of citizenship, both above and below the level of the nation state, have been totally renewed.

References

Badie, B., Brauman, R., Decaux, E., Devin, G., & Wihtol de Wenden, C. (2008). *Pour un autre regard sur les migrations: Construire une gouvernance globale*. La découverte.
Bauböck, R. (1994). *Transnational citizenship: Membership and rights in international migration*. Edward Elgar.
Bauman, Z. (2000). *Liquid modernity*. Cambridge University Press.
Bertossi, C., & Wihtol de Wenden, C. (2007). *Les couleurs du drapeau: L'armée française face aux discriminations*. Robert Laffont.
Body-Gendrot, S., & Wihtol de Wenden, C. (2014). *Policing the inner cities in France, the United Kingdom and the United States*. Palgrave/Pivot.
Brubaker, R. (2000). *Citoyenneté et nationalité en France et en Allemagne*. Belin.
Castles, S. (1997). Multicultural citizenship: A response to the dilemma of globalisation and national identity. *Journal of Intercultural Studies, 18*(1), 5–23.
Castles, S., & Davidson, A. (2000). *Citizenship and migration: Globalisation and the politics of belonging*. Macmillan.
Cesari, J. (1994). *Être musulman en France*. Karthala.
Etienne, B. (1989). *La France et l'Islam*. Hachette.
Hammar, T. (1990). *Democracy and the nation state: Aliens, denizens, and citizens in a world of international migration*. Avebury.

Hirschman, A. (1970). *Exit, voice and loyalty: Responses to decline in firms, organisations and states*. Harvard University Press.

Kepel, G. (1987). *Les banlieues de l'Islam*. Le Seuil.

Kymlicka, W. (1995). *Multicultural citizenship: A liberal theory of minority rights*. Oxford University Press.

Lavisse, E. (2014). *Histoire de France*. Armand Colin.

Leveau, R., & Mohsen, K. (Eds.). (2005). *Musulmans de France et d'Europe*. CNRS Editions.

Leveau, R., & Wihtol de Wenden, C. (2001). *La beurgeoisie: Les trois âges de la vie associative issue de l'immigration*. CNRS Editions.

Rex, J., & Singh, G. (Eds.). (2004). *The governance of multiculturalism*. Ashgate.

Safran, W. (1991). Diasporas in modern societies: Myths of homeland and return. *Diaspora, 1*(1), 83–99.

Sayad, A. (1999). *La double absence*. Seuil.

Scheffer, G. (2006). *Diaspora politics: At home abroad*. Cambridge University Press.

Soysal, Y. (1994). *The limits of citizenship: Migrants and post-colonial citizenship in Europe*. Chicago University Press.

Weil, P. (2004). *Qu'est-ce qu'un Français? Histoire de la nationalité française depuis la Révolution*. Gallimard.

Wieviorka, M. (1994). *Racisme et xénophobie en Europe: Une comparaison internationale*. La découverte.

Wihtol de Wenden, C. (1997). *La Citoyenneté européenne*. Presses de Sciences Po.

Wihtol de Wenden, C. (2004). Multiculturalism in France. In J. Rex & G. Singh (Eds.), *The governance of multiculturalism*. Ashgate.

Wihtol de Wenden, C. (2013). *Le droit d'émigrer*. CNRS Editions.

Wihtol de Wenden, C. (2017). *La question migratoire au XXIème siècle: Migrants, réfugiés et relations internationales*. Presses de Sciences Po.

Open Access This chapter is licensed under the terms of the Creative Commons Attribution 4.0 International License (http://creativecommons.org/licenses/by/4.0/), which permits use, sharing, adaptation, distribution and reproduction in any medium or format, as long as you give appropriate credit to the original author(s) and the source, provide a link to the Creative Commons license and indicate if changes were made.

The images or other third party material in this chapter are included in the chapter's Creative Commons license, unless indicated otherwise in a credit line to the material. If material is not included in the chapter's Creative Commons license and your intended use is not permitted by statutory regulation or exceeds the permitted use, you will need to obtain permission directly from the copyright holder.

Chapter 5
Migration Diplomacy and Multi-actor Governance

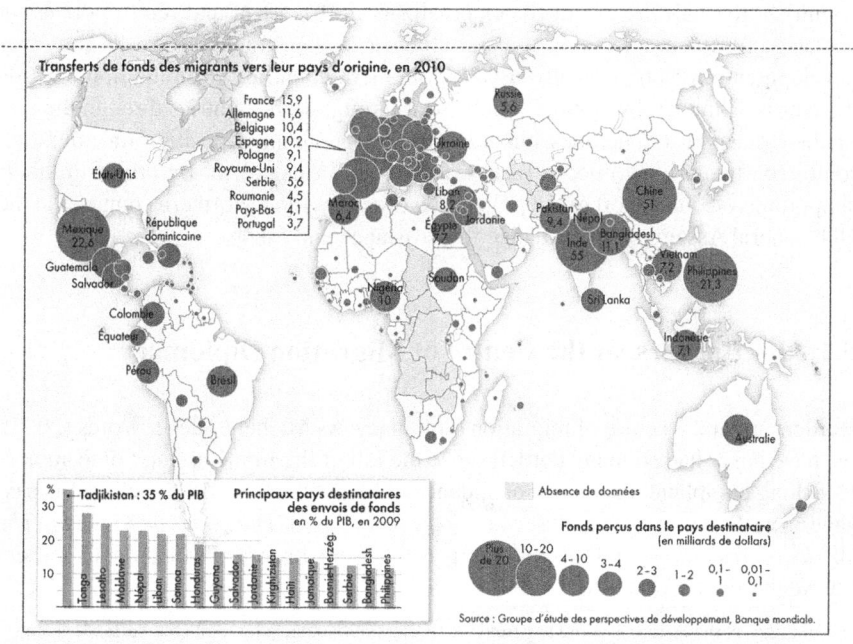

Remittances sent by migrants to their countries of departure (in billion dollars)
Americas: Canada, USA, Mexico, Guatemala, Salvador, Colombia, Equator, Dominican Republic, Peru, Bolivia, Brazil
Europe: France, Germany, Belgium, Italy, Spain, Romania, Poland, Hungary, Portugal, Serbia, United Kingdom, Check Republic, Austria, Sweden, Russia, Uzbekistan
Africa: Morocco, Nigeria, Egypt, South Sudan, Kenya
Middle East: Turkey, Jordanian, Yemen, Lebanon
Pakistan, India, Nepal, Bangladesh, Sri Lanka, China, Thailand, Vietnam, Philippines, Indonesia, South Korea, Japan

Various forms of migration diplomacy have now developed, which make use of several tools. This typically involves bilateral and multilateral agreements regarding the externalisation of borders and the provision of visas for highly-skilled migrants from the Global South in exchange for the repatriation of undocumented migrants and the creation of new development policies. Countries of origin have also adopted new strategies in this domain, including adopting a greater openness towards dual citizenship, allowing national voting rights for migrants in their countries of origin (notably in Latin America), developing remittance policies, supporting diasporic associations, and promoting their elites abroad. Migration diplomacy is also conducted at the regional and global level, including in contexts of free circulation at the regional level. New actors advocating for migrants' rights and human rights are also emerging at the global level.

Migration diplomacy is not only a strategy developed by Northern immigration countries, through the use of the externalization of borders and return policies in exchange for the provision of visas for elites or the construction of roads and other development projects. It is also used by Southern countries of emigration towards the North, who thereby attempt to influence immigration countries through the size of their diaspora (sometimes binational), their geographic position on migration routes (particularly Morocco, Turkey, Libya, and Mexico), or by promising their support to vote in support of the policies favoured by some Northern countries at the UN General Assembly, in exchange for assistance and funds.

5.1   I – Borders, at the Centre of Migration Diplomacy

Borders are at the centre of migration diplomacy. As Michel Foucher writes (2007), we have never had so many borders since the fall of the Iron Curtain. Some authors have long complained about the abundance of borders in the world, such as this passage from Stefan Zweig's 1942 autobiographical work *Die Welt von Gestern* (*The World of Yesterday*; 1993), comparing his present historical situation to the era before the First World War:

> Nothing, perhaps, makes more apparent the tremendous setback the world has suffered since the First World War than the restrictions now placed on the freedom of movement of men and, in general, on their rights [...]. There were no permits, no visas, no cumbersome procedures; the same borders which, with their customs officers, police and gendarmerie posts, have been transformed into a system of obstacles, represented nothing more than symbolic lines which were crossed with as much thoughtlessness as the Greenwich meridian.

The proliferation of border crossings poses a challenge for the policies and diplomatic positions of nation states faced with large migration flows: "harraga" (migrants from North Africa who burn their identity papers) are "burning" borders, and while countries of origin conclude agreements with immigration countries to prohibit illegal departures, human smugglers continue to offer expensive and dangerous routes of entry, transnational networks facilitate border crossings by means of family, economic, cultural, or social links, and dual citizenship is used as a means to bypass visas systems. All borders are challenged by various forms of transnationalism, because the will of individuals looking for a better future, for asylum, or for jobs is stronger than the will of military troops to close borders. Nation states that are afraid of the disorder that might result from migrants crossing their borders are mostly adopting the approach of externalising their borders. However, other forms of diplomacy are being practised on a large scale, while city networks and other transnational mobilisations are also emerging as new actors in opposition to security-based approaches.

5.1.1 Bilateral and Multilateral Agreements

Many bilateral and multilateral agreements have been concluded between individual emigration and immigration countries (bilateral agreements), or between groups of countries (multilateral agreements).

The EU-Turkey agreement of March 2016 included Turkey's acceptance to host the majority of refugees from Syria and other Middle Eastern countries in exchange for €6 billion and increased international recognition. Some of Turkey's other demands, such as its application to work towards membership of the EU and the simplification of visas for Turkish people travelling to Europe, were not granted. The border between Calais and Dover continues to be managed according to the Touquet agreements, which were concluded between the UK and France in 2002. According to the terms of these agreements, France controls the borders in an effort to stop irregular migrants or asylum seekers from reaching the UK. This is the only situation in which a European country controls the border for another, at departure rather than at arrival. This task of containment is more often demanded of countries in the Global South. The management of this border is often a cause of conflict between France and the UK, despite the fact that the encampment of migrants near Calais, the so-called "jungle", has been cleared several times (2002, 2009, and 2016), before being reconstructed by newcomers, and despite the cold reception that awaits them on the other side. The border between Ceuta and Melilla, and the geographical position of Morocco across the Mediterranean Sea from Europe, has been used by Morocco to negotiate many bilateral agreements with EU Member States, but not multilateral ones with the whole EU, since Morocco does not want to damage its relations with Western African countries. These negotiations are leading to a kind of thick border covering the whole country, owing to the requirement imposed by EU Member States to control the whole Moroccan territory. Libya took advantage of its long southern Mediterranean shore to conclude the largest number of bilateral and multilateral agreements with European countries, in exchange for millions of euros, infrastructure projects, and recognition of its legitimacy on the international scene during the Gaddafi period until 2011 (he was officially invited by French and Italian governments). For countries in the Global South, these agreements have led to increased recognition in the North, and an opportunity to better equip their internal security forces.

The externalisation of European borders has been extended to the domain of asylum control. Many EU Member States are sub-contracting their asylum procedures to third countries at the external borders of Europe, with which they conclude readmission agreements in exchange for development policies, various kinds of external cooperation, and visas for elites. France has concluded the greatest number of readmission agreements of any EU Member State, followed by Italy, the UK,

Switzerland, and Sweden. Each country has chosen a distinct approach. During the 1990s, bilateral agreements were mostly concluded with Eastern European countries, including Albania and Ukraine, before the admission of some of those countries into the EU. Conditional negotiations were conducted with Balkan countries. From 2002 to 2018, these agreements were extended to Africa, with a wide range of working arrangements or partnerships, combining security, humanitarian missions, development, and trade. However, the approach of externalising borders is mostly used for containment and deterrence at the point of departure.

Recently, the externalization of borders has been extended to the domain of asylum policies, with some Northern immigration countries in Europe (the UK, Sweden, and Denmark) trying to assess candidates for asylum while they are still in their countries of origin or in transit countries. In this context, Rwanda, in the Great Lakes region of Central Africa, was chosen for its political and economic stability to be a partner for these countries. This approach aims to avoid the arrival of mixed flows in Northern countries, so that "true" candidates for asylum can be identified, instead of the usual blurring of categories leading to large numbers of irregular migrants. Although this practice contravenes the Geneva Convention of 1951 on asylum, which requires that candidates for asylum be granted access to the asylum country, it has become a popular idea in European and national debates.

5.2 II – International Conventions and Declarations

The term "governance" is generally understood as a "broad concept that refers to mechanisms for steering systems towards their goals", in which states are one of many competing sources of authority, along with other multilateral actors. For James Rosenau (1990), governance also refers to a global level, where transnational issues require hybrid forms of cooperation between disparate types of actors. It came to be applied to migration management in a context of great disorder and violation of human rights, when migration gradually came to be viewed as a world issue. This situation of confusion, the manifest discrepancies between objectives and results, and the perverse effects of some national policies all called for a global system of governance.

During the 1990s, several specialists of migration focused their books on the "global migration crisis" (Weiner, 1995) and on nation states "losing control" of borders (Sassen, 1996b), while others emphasised the contradiction between the contribution that mobility brings to human development and the closure of borders by visas systems across two-thirds of the planet, or highlighted the emerging demand for a right to emigrate and to practise mobility, as a world public good, in a world that is currently restricting that mobility. The gaps between policy objectives and their manifest failures led to the idea that migration would be better managed at a larger level than that of the nation state. Earlier attempts to develop mechanisms of global governance for issues with a global dimension (the environment, population issues, women's rights, etc.) suggested that such mechanisms could be enlarged to address migration.

At the global level, migration is approached as a matter of international relations. There are a number of universal declarations and international treaties relating to migration: the Universal Declaration of Human Rights of 1948 says that every human being has the right to leave a country, including one's own. The Geneva Convention of 1951 protects refugees and defines the necessary criteria for being granted this status. While refugees have universal protection from the Geneva Convention of 1951, which was first written to apply only to Europeans, then enlarged in 1967 and 1969 to extend to the whole world, migrants lack such general and universal rights, because they are governed by the laws of immigration states, which define rights of entry, work, and settlement at the national level. Most countries in the Global South do not have any immigration nor refugee policies, and few of them are signatories of the International Convention on Refugees (1951), or of those on statelessness (1954), equality of social rights at work with nationals (ILO resolutions N° 97 and 143), or children's rights (1989). In 1990, after ten years of work, the United Nations invited Member States to sign the 1990 International Convention on the Protection of the Rights of all Migrant Workers and Members of their Families (ICRMW). This convention, now signed by 56 countries – all from the Global South except for Kosovo and Montenegro – does not provide any innovations or access to new rights. It simply refers to all rights already existing in the world for migrant workers, while granting some minimum rights to irregular migrants. For this reason, no immigration country of the Global North has signed the Convention. However, Southern countries who signed this convention with the aim of protecting their nationals abroad often encounter difficulties when they are themselves confronted with immigrants, as new immigration countries.

5.2.1 *Towards an International Governance of Migration*

Since 2003, the idea that migration would be better managed at a larger level than the nation state began to emerge in Geneva, with the Geneva Migration Group of experts.

The project to develop a system for the global governance of migration was launched by Kofi Annan, General Secretary of the United Nations in 2006 (Badie et al., 2008). He was interested in a process undertaken in Geneva in 2003 by several international organisations and NGOs, which aimed to open up a broader reflection on migration (the GMG, "Geneva Migration Group", and later "Global Migration Group", established in 2003, which rapidly gathered 17 participant organisations). In 2016 Kofi Annan undertook to create a High Level Dialogue at the United Nations headquarters in New York, followed by annual meetings of the Global Forum on Migration and Development in Brussels (2007), Manilla (2008), Athens (2009), Puerto Vallarta (2010), Geneva (2011), Mauritius (2012), Stockholm (2014), Istanbul (2015), and Berlin (2017). The United Nations organised a second High level Dialogue in New York in 2013.

The main idea behind this project is to draw on a larger body of expertise and to create space for multilateralism as a decision-making process. The ineffectiveness of national border controls, in spite of security-based discourses and practices and the violation of human rights in virtually every operation, progressively led to the idea that a supranational level of decision-making would be capable of taking account of more contradictory factors and ethical principles than decision-making at the national level, which is embroiled in national politics and public opinion, and therefore tends towards security-based discourses. The Global Forum on Migration and Development is a work in progress, whose reflections are based principally on the ICRMW. However, the Forum has only limited legitimacy on the international scene, as the High Level Dialogue itself does not belong to the sphere of international diplomacy, but rather to that of parallel practices.

In 2015, after the refugee crisis, the UN National Assembly decided to launch a Global Compact for Migration and a Global Compact on Refugees, with the aim of establishing (through the multilateral decision-making process of global governance) a non-binding text that most countries could agree on, to be followed as a framework. The topic had never been placed on the agenda of any world conference of the United Nations before (the issue of "population" was debated in Cairo in 1994, "women" in Beijing in 1998, and "discrimination" in Durban in 2002). The topic of migration had not even been debated at G8 meetings or at the UN National Assembly before 2015. The reason for this is a lack of transnational mobilisation on issues of migration and refugees. Those who are in favour of opening borders are emigration states (mostly signatories of the UN Convention of 1990), associations of migrants involved in the development of their countries of origin, human rights organisations, and large companies seeking sources of labour force. These actors have no tradition of fighting in transnational mobilisations together – a fact which weakens the project to develop a global governance of migration. Aristide Zolberg names the actors in such mobilisations "strange bedfellows" (Zolberg, 2006): for example, while employers may share the goals of leftist or charity activists who support the opening of borders, they otherwise have little in common. Similarly, defenders of welfare provisions may share the goals of nationalists who support the closure of borders, but are otherwise very different in their views.

The Global Compact was opened to signatories at the end of 2018, with the aim of facilitating "safe, orderly, and regular migration". It defines a roadmap to be followed for migrants and refugees respectively. However, immigration states continue to be reluctant to implement the Global Compact, which specifies 23 objectives (with regard to migration) to be followed by the General Assembly of the UN and 4 main points (with regard to refugees) to be followed by UNHCR.

The global governance of migration involves immigration and emigration states from the Global North and Global South, IGOs, NGOs, the EU, and many actors from civil society: trade unions, migrants' associations, human rights organisations, churches, associations for local development, experts, and all other such actors involved in migration and refugee issues. Southern countries are now active participants in the debate. Some of them are emerging immigration and transit states (such as Turkey, Morocco, and Mexico). These states are developing forms of soft diplomacy that capitalise on this new position and establish diasporic policies towards their emigrants, demanding rights for them in their immigration states. Through these new kinds of soft diplomacy they are beginning to have a voice in World Social Forums, FMMD annual meetings, and in the Global Compact.

Some small states are gaining a voice thanks to their advocacy on environmental issues or regarding the treatment of their nationals abroad ("indigenous work"). For example, Bangladesh has developed these sorts of "soft diplomacy" thanks to the support of experts. Meanwhile, a number of issues that have a strong impact on migration and which could more effectively be debated at the global level have not yet been put on the agenda, such as the price of cotton, extensive fishing in African waters by Asian countries, open markets in raw materials, and demography.

However, in the future, the disorder of the world will be addressed by new forms of international relations, which will be more socially-orientated, with a larger role for the Global South, and less dependent on nation states of the Global North as the main actors of international relations. As Bertrand Badie observes: "We are analyzing migration questions in terms of inter-state relations, whereas the world system no longer works this way" (Badie, 2022). At the global level, social issues are becoming more important than strategic ones. At the international level, the social question is becoming the foremost factor in the destabilisation of the world, owing to inequalities in human development, poverty, civil wars, environmental crises, and demography. The forces of globalisation are creating relations of interdependency, which contradict the principles of sovereignty. The pressures associated with societies are often stronger than those associated with states, and this reality is highlighted by the patterns of migration flows. International relations are also being shaped by the effects of global pandemics, whereas they would previously have been dominated by relations of military power. Migration flows are a manifestation of the changing dynamics of societies, as they emerge in ways that seek to limit inequalities, fill gaps, and reciprocally satisfy new needs. The project to establish the rules of this new global order requires the recognition of migration as a legitimate factor in the debate, which has not yet been accomplished.

Recent crises (the Syrian civil war, COVID-19, and war in Afghanistan) have revealed a large gap between, on the one hand, the objectives of multilateral methods of governance connected with the Marrakech Global Compact, and on the other hand, European and national solutions to new migration and refugee flows. The only way to resolve these questions is by establishing legal channels of mobility for greater numbers of migrants.

5.3 III – From Local to Global: Cities as New Actors in International Migration

Other transnational mobilisations are also entering the field of international advocacy and questioning the role of nation states. Owing to the increasing urbanisation of the planet, cities are becoming important territories of departure and arrival. During the past thirty years, some major cities have hosted informal markets for newcomers, such as Berlin and Vienna after the fall of the Berlin wall in 1989, and Istanbul, with its informal markets for circular migration. There is a diverse range of actors involved in the management of cities in relation to migration: the EU, with its regulation of circulation, municipalities, humanitarian NGOs, associations, and citizens involved in receiving migrants and lobbying public decision-makers. The cases of Palermo, Barcelona, Strasburg, and other cities are well-known. Small cities are also involved, but citizens who decide to provide hospitality to irregular migrants or help them cross borders often find themselves in contravention of the law. There has been an increase in these "crimes of solidarity". One such high profile case was that of Cédric Herrou, a farmer in the French Alps, who was prosecuted and found guilty for his role in assisting irregular migrants, before the cases against him were overturned by the Constitutional Council, the Highest Court in France, on the basis that such actions of "fraternity" (one of the founding values of the French Republic, alongside freedom and equality) are protected by the Constitution. This story was documented in a film, *Libre,* produced after the successful resolution of Herrou's court cases. The legal cases involving Domenico Lucano, the mayor of Riace in Italy, and those of the inhabitants of Briançon, are bringing to light contradictions between legal justice and ethics.

In some places, the work of receiving migrants with the help of NGOs, and sometimes with European funds, can be an opportunity to create jobs in solidarity management. This work combines the public and private sectors, and often takes place in regions of unemployment or rural depopulation, such as in Sicily (Bassi, 2015), the Nord-Pas de Calais region in France, or on Greek islands. Cities are also initiating civil society solidarity networks with migrants, involving mobilisation at the local, grass-roots level, aimed at supporting unaccompanied minors, irregular migrants, asylum seekers, and families.

Cities may also develop networks on an international scale when they are involved in environmental crises, such as Dacca in Bangladesh and others located at sea level, such as Mumbai, Kolkata, or New Orleans in the wake of Storm Katrina (Gemenne et al., 2016). Some international agreements between Northern and Southern cities involved in immigration and emigration respectively have also aimed at developing better forms of management in Southern societies confronted with the challenges of rapid urbanisation. These co-development agreements address issues such as waste treatment, access to clean water, urban social housing, uses of remittances, and the improvement of daily life in urban areas as well as in rural ones.

The forces of both globalisation and localism are therefore revealing new facets of cities and migration, in ways that bring to mind Immanuel Kant's emphasis on hospitality as a universal duty of a citizen in a cosmopolitan world, followed by Zygmunt Bauman's concept of liquid modernity (Wihtol de Wenden, 2013, referring to Kant, 2006; Bauman, 2000).

5.3.1 Cities as International Networks

In the mid-1990s, Saskia Sassen's (1996a) work on the "global city" drew attention to the weakening of nation states and the strengthening of transnational networks in economics, finance, and trade, using the examples of London, New York, and

Tokyo. This "local turn" was also examined by authors including Peter Scholten (2015) and Bianca Garces-Mascarenas and Rinus Penninx (2015) in the Netherlands, focusing on the role of cities in implementing migration and integration policies and processes in Europe. These works raise the question of the role of cities in migrations flows and the construction of networks beyond the level of nation states, and thus their role in integration policies and global governance at all levels of scale. In their book on city networks, Thomas Lacroix and Sarah Spencer (2022) ask the question: will cities come to govern the world with regard to integration policies and the global governance of migration, in place of national and international policies? The perspective of governance from below, studied at the meso-level of city networks, is a good place to observe the large diversity of situations, thanks to the emergence of new actors and new fields in connection with cities.

Little research has been devoted to cities in relation to migration policies, either as actors involved in the reception of migrants, or as experts in governance from below (at multi-scale levels) in reaction to national and international policies imposed from above. In her work on multilevel decision-making processes, Tiziana Caponio (2022) emphasises the ambiguous, horizontal dimension of meso-level governance. She writes that the horizontal level of towns as new actors of migration policies at the local, national, and international level has been "poorly conceptualized" and effectively considered as being subordinated to vertical, intergovernmental relations of only secondary relevance. The collaborative, multilevel, and inter-sectorial governance found in connection with cities can be analysed from several perspectives, including those of networks, activists, and the structuring role of the political context on cities in their migration strategy.

5.3.2 *Smart Cities and Cities of Marginalisation*

While some global cities have been termed "smart cities", attracting highly qualified migrants from all over the world, they are also creating cosmopolitan forms of citizenship beyond nation states by receiving newcomers from poor countries and lower social categories. In his work on the reception of migrants, Michel Agier quotes Jacques Derrida (2019, p. 84):

> If we refer to the city rather than the state, is it because we hope to receive from a new figure of the city that which we have almost given up expecting from the state. [...] What we call (calling it what we would wish it to be) the "city of refuge" is no longer simply a set of new attributes or new powers added to a classic and unchanged concept of the city. It is no longer just a question of new predicates to enhance the old subject called "the city". No, we are dreaming of another concept, another law, another policy for the city.

In France, urban policy has been at the centre of integration policies since the 1990s, but this situation was conceived as the implementation of national policy at the local level, with few international outputs, and without cities being actors of these policies. The arrival of large numbers of refugees, first in 2011 and then with the so called "refugee crisis" of 2015, brought about a significant shift. The questions then arose of the role of cities in affecting the reception of migrants, and of the effects of migrants on the city. These cities have witnessed the emergence of informal practices, significant numbers of residents of irregular status, many cases of passage without settlement, and the continuation of provisional ways of life, together with practices of hospitality from below.

The city is central to the development of migration, since, at the global level, migration is closely related to the increasing urbanisation of the planet (in particular it is predicted that the population of Africa will change from being 70% rural in 1950 to being 70% urban in 2050). Urban residents are generally more educated, more open to new technologies of information and communication, and also more vulnerable to the offers of human smugglers owing to their dream of a future abroad. They may be attracted by global cities, but then effectively come to reside at the margins of those cities. As Saskia Sassen (2014) demonstrates, most poor migrants are effectively excluded from cities, relegated to living in camps (Agier, 2014), border cities, transit zones, slums, or deprived inner-city areas. This process is accelerated by the difficulties that migrants experience in obtaining legal access and status in the course of their travels, leading to the creation of new peripheries which hardly look like cities (such as the camps or "jungles" described by Michel Agier). The sorts of "transit zones" housing "transmigrants" studied by Alain Tarrius (2010) and Anaïk Pian (2009), such as those in Morocco or Calais (the so called "jungle"), are often dismantled but always rebuilt. Border cities such as Tijuana in Mexico or El Paso have also seen the emergence of ghettos, in which communities reconstruct their former ways of life.

5.3.3 Sanctuary Cities and Welcoming Cities

The growth in the role of cities in migration has also led to the emergence of "sanctuary cities" and "welcoming cities", in which hospitality is conceived in terms of networks of solidarity. Urban actors have diversified themselves. Notable examples include Strasburg, Barcelona, and Palermo, which was named a cosmopolitan city by its mayor Leoluca Orlando. Another case is that of Riace, a town in Puglia in Southern Italy, where the mayor, Domenico Lucano, was prohibited from staying in his own town by the state, and then charged with allowing newly arrived undocumented migrants to work in cooperatives in order to help them to settle and integrate. Grande-Synthe, a suburb of Dunkirk, which was led by its mayor Damien Carême until his election to the European Parliament in 2020, similarly tried to find another way of receiving newcomers, in opposition to the behaviour of some mayors and local authorities. He created the association ANVITA (Association Nationale des Villes et Territoires Accueillants, which gathers participants from 53 territories). Meanwhile, in Belgium, the "Communes hospitalières" network includes 126 participant towns and villages, and across Europe 747 such "welcoming cities" can be now be found. These endeavours are helped by the emergence of civil society solidarity networks devoted to assisting irregular migrants, focusing on pragmatic solutions to a sensitive multilevel governance issue.

In some cases, efforts to develop cities' hospitality to newcomers are motivated not only by ethical concerns but also by the desire to create employment in the fields of expertise and the management of associations for migrants, in contexts of nationwide unemployment. This may be funded at the local, national, or European level, and would not be possible without the arrival of newcomers. In Lyons, Nantes, and Strasburg, local authorities have been involved in the development of migration-related city networks. Strasburg was granted the status of "welcoming city" ("ville accueillante") in 2018, partly thanks to the establishment of a council for long-term settled foreigners. Some cities faced with large refugee flows, such as Grande-Synthe, Saint-Denis (near Paris), Lyon, and Briançon have had to cope with the dismantling of settlements and conflicts between activists devoted to welcoming migrants (who may be prosecuted for "crimes of solidarity") and the police. Meanwhile, refugees in this context face difficult decisions between staying, going back, or continuing on their journeys. The network of welcoming cities is now a world network, with a global parliament of mayors and 14 networks of refuge towns.

In Germany, some towns played a crucial role in welcoming refugees during the 2015 refugee crisis (Hinger, 2021), either as a complement or as alternatives to actions carried out by the state, with the help of citizens in their homes. These towns and the networks of social relations that they developed became a driving force for improving the governance of immigration. In this federal country, towns exercise some autonomy in implementing integration policies and European recommendations at the local level. With the help of non-profit associations such as Caritas, they participated in resettlement programs for refugees and contributed to opening the labour market to refugees and asylum seekers, in order to avoid them falling into a so-called "duldung" *s*tatus (in which they are neither granted a legal status, nor expelled), thus separating social issues from the issue of migrants' legal status. In Berlin, the city subsidised housing for each applicant at a rate of €750 per month. In the city of Halle, the town rented 700 flats for newcomers, as it made a priority of guaranteeing that there was housing for everyone. In this country, immigration was not a principal topic of debate during the elections for a new chancellor after Angela Merkel.

City networks can also include universities, which can facilitate network socialisation through knowledge exchange regarding integration and inclusion. As policy agents, city networks help to formulate and implement immigration and integration policies.

5.3.4 *Cities Are New Actors in Transnational Projects*

In the Mediterranean region, large cities have created transnational and international networks of knowledge and migration management. Ricard Zapata-Barrero et al. (2017) speak about "the local turn" in migration governance, in which

Mediterranean cities acting "from below" have created resilient regional networks. Taking the example of Barcelona, he shows that global cities' experience of migration settlement has led to opportunities to relocate governance in the Mediterranean region from states to cities (for example, through the Euro-Mediterranean Partnership, the Charter of Palermo of 2015, and the Palermo/Izmir Partnership) but also to address the management of irregular migration, unaccompanied minors, and asylum seekers. A new way of thinking emerged, based on the construction of networks across the Mediterranean region, and in which cities can be a focus for promoting alternative forms of regional migration governance, while also taking account of the Global Compact Agenda 2030 for sustainable development.

Cities are also developing networks between the Global South and Global North, giving rise to city-based forms of diplomacy and decentralised cooperation, which can avoid the polarisation typical of national debates and conflicts between migrant associations and local elites in the South. These networks also tend to promote goals of human development in preference to the approaches favoured by Western development models. Some examples in Senegal and Mali, facilitated by their diasporas and migrant associations, are focused on achieving autonomy at the local level in preference to the national level, in order to promote local development in regions of emigration and demonstrate good practice (according to UNDP recommendations).

At a larger scale, big cities can also become subjects of international relations when they are involved in facing huge international challenges, such as environment challenges. They take on a global dimension when they are victims of environmental crises and when they become the focus of major international problems. If sea levels continue to rise, many big cities situated at sea level, particularly in Asia, will see larger numbers of environmentally displaced persons and many deaths, primarily among the poorest, who have more limited options for internal mobility within their country (for example, in Dacca, Kolkata, and Mumbai). No internal status exists for environmentally displaced persons, and this fact led Bangladesh to develop, with the support of experts, an approach of soft diplomacy in the UN, aimed at advocating for the future needs of those large cities, even though this approach has not yet yielded obvious benefits (Baillat, 2015). The experience of New Orleans in the wake of Hurricane Katrina is also emblematic in this regard: the poorest stayed in place, owing to a lack of resources, while others left for other regions of the US, although the city made efforts to move parts of its population. The policy response to this disaster involved the national (federal) state, the state of Louisiana, and the city (Gemenne et al., 2016). Multilevel analysis is particularly relevant in such a case.

Networks of large cities are also creating further mobilisations by moving policy-making to different political levels. The rising importance of cities as international actors has had an impact on the Global Compact for Migration at the global level. Cities have also organised themselves through associations and networks involved in knowledge exchange and action aimed at redefining governance, such as through the role of individual mayors as global leaders (for example, at the Mayoral Forum 2014 and the GCM 2018 in Marrakech), through city mobilisation in response to the humanitarian needs of vulnerable migrants, and through agreements between cities as a means of providing channels for inter-state mobility. The impact of migration therefore appears at the local, national, and international level. Migration policy has an influence on various levels of governance, as can be seen, for example, in the context of the COVID-19 pandemic, when coalitions of towns, cities, and nation states emerged to protect the undocumented. Cities and mayors are involved in addressing climate issues, the challenges of urbanisation, the implementation of the GCM, and in facilitating cooperative localism, anti-discrimination practices, and the strengthening of networks (Thouez, 2022). In a context in which traditional actors of civil society have declined – such as trade unions, churches, and even companies – cities are now welcoming migrants, although entry policies remain the remit of nation states. Non-state actors have acquired significant, and sometimes crucial roles thanks to the practice of multilateralism, including the proliferation of partnerships with non-state actors. Thanks to city networking (including contacts between universities, activists, and migrants), horizontal forces are strengthening and developing transnationalism, multilevel forms of governance, knowledge exchange, and new abilities to work in emergency situations.

5.4 Conclusion

The development of migration diplomacy is drawing attention to the role of new actors: emigration countries of the Global South, city networks, transnational mobilisations, diasporic associations, and networks for supporting elites abroad. It is also producing a wide range of outputs: bilateral and multilateral agreements, development policies, dual citizenship agreements, voting rights in countries of origin and of settlement, and remittance policies. In immigration countries, most of these outputs are the result of multilevel decision-making, involving actors from the local to the global level, since migration diplomacy has also been conducted at the global level, through the development of forms of global migration governance.

Some recent examples illustrate the role that migration diplomacy has played, in situations where emigration states have influenced migration management and border policies in the Global North. Just before the closure of borders owing to the COVID-19 pandemic, in January and February 2020, Turkey decided to open its borders with Greece to refugees settled in Turkey, because it considered that, although the EU had paid the funds that it had reluctantly agreed to, the two other conditions demanded by Turkey in the EU/Turkey agreements of 2016 had not been fulfilled: the simplification of visas for Turks travelling to Europe and the re-examination of Turkey's application to join the EU. Consequently, migrants could freely travel by bus to the Greek border, until the COVID-19 crisis led to the closure of the border and the repatriation of Syrians in Turkey. Another manifestation of the struggle between emigration states and EU Member States was the disagreement between Morocco and Spain in summer 2021: as Spain had received an activist belonging to the Polisario movement (contesting Moroccan settlement of the

Western Sahara region inhabited by Sahrawi populations), Morocco retaliated by opening the borders of Ceuta and Melilla to Moroccan migrants wishing to travel to Spain. Perhaps the clearest example of such migration diplomacy is the decision of Belarus to attract Middle Eastern migrants to its border with Poland in winter 2021, as a way of applying pressure on the EU, which had been critical of the country's government. This attempt to use migrants and refugees as bargaining chips resulted in many people struggling to survive in swamps and snow in the depths of winter, while trying to cross the Polish border and seek refuge.

Another aspect of migration as diplomacy has emerged from the development of a transnational movement of religious diplomacy centred on Islam since the 1980. Although organisations such as the Muslim Brotherhood are informal and asymmetric actors in relation to nation states and international geopolitics, Islamic radicalisation has proved to be an influential force in the construction of threats to security, and Islam has been used as a tool in strategies of alliances and conflicts.

References

Agier, M. (2014). *Un monde de camps*. La découverte.
Agier, M. (2019). *L'étranger qui vient*. Gallimard.
Badie, B. (2022, November 16–17). Conference. Grenoble Institute of Political Studies.
Badie, B., Brauman, R., Decaux, E., Devin, G., & Wihtol de Wenden, C. (2008). *Pour un autre regard sur les migrations: Construire une gouvernance globale*. La découverte.
Baillat, A. (2015). *The soft diplomacy of poor nation states: Bangladesh involved in environmental risks* [Doctoral thesis, Sciences Po].
Bassi, M. (2015). Politiques de contrôle et gestion des réalités locales dans la gestion des migrations indésirables en Sicile. In C. Schmoll, H. Thiollet, & C. Wihtol de Wenden (Eds.), *Migrations en Méditerranée* (pp. 157–167). CNRS Editions.
Bauman, Z. (2000). *Liquid modernity*. Cambridge University Press.
Caponio, T. (2022). Scaling migration network governance? City networks and civil society in multilevel policymaking dynamics. *Global Networks, 22*, 397–412. https://doi.org/10.1111/glob.12263
Foucher, M. (2007). *L'obsession des frontières*. Perrin.
Garces-Mascarenas, B., & Penninx, R. (2015). *Integration processes and policies in Europe* (IMISCOE research series). Springer.
Gemenne, F., Ionesco, D., & Mokhachevna, D. (2016). *Atlas des migrations environnementales*. Presses de Sciences Po.
Hinger, S. (2021). Paper at conference at CERI organised by Thomas Lacroix on "Cities and Migration", 10/9/2021.
Kant, I. (2006). *Projet de paix perpétuelle*. Nathan.
Lacroix, T., & Spencer, S. (Eds.). (2022). Special issue: Cities in networks. *Global networks* (Vol. 22, issue 3).
Pian, A. (2009). *Aux nouvelles frontières de l'Europe: L'aventure incertaine des Sénégalais au Maroc*. La dispute.
Rosenau, J. (1990). *Turbulence in world politics*. Princeton University Press.
Sassen, S. (1996a). *La Ville globale*. Descartes et Cie.
Sassen, S. (1996b). *Losing control? Sovereignty in an age of globalisation*. Columbia University Press.
Sassen, S. (2014). *Expulsions: Brutality and complexity in the global economy*. Belknap Press.

References

Scholten, P. (2015). *Integrating immigrants in Europe* (IMISCOE research series). Springer.

Tarrius, A. (2010). *Migrants internationaux et nouveaux réseaux criminels*. Trabucaire.

Thouez, C. (2022). New power configurations: City mobilization and policy change. *Global Networks, 22*(3), 363–376.

Weiner, M. (1995). *The global migration crisis: Challenges to states and to human rights*. Harper and Collins.

Wihtol de Wenden, C. (2013). *Le droit d'émigrer*. CNRS Editions.

Zapata-Barrero, R., Caponio, T., & Scholten, P. (2017). Theorizing the local turn in a multi-level governance framework of analysis: A case study in immigrant policies. *International Review of Administrative Sciences, 83*(2), 241–246.

Zolberg, A. (2006). *A nation by design: Immigration policy and the fashioning of America*. Cambridge University Press.

Open Access This chapter is licensed under the terms of the Creative Commons Attribution 4.0 International License (http://creativecommons.org/licenses/by/4.0/), which permits use, sharing, adaptation, distribution and reproduction in any medium or format, as long as you give appropriate credit to the original author(s) and the source, provide a link to the Creative Commons license and indicate if changes were made.

The images or other third party material in this chapter are included in the chapter's Creative Commons license, unless indicated otherwise in a credit line to the material. If material is not included in the chapter's Creative Commons license and your intended use is not permitted by statutory regulation or exceeds the permitted use, you will need to obtain permission directly from the copyright holder.

Chapter 6
Migration and Development

The topic of the relationship between migration and development is one of the most controversial areas in migration research and policy. For a long time, it was considered that development was an alternative to migration, because in European history, emigration flows from Southern European countries came to an end when those countries experienced economic growth and developed more democratic political systems. In Spain, Portugal, Italy, and Greece, migration decreased or disappeared around the time of their entry into the EU. However, the assumption that the same patterns will emerge in countries on the southern rim of the Mediterranean Sea runs into several problems. The first problem relates to the demographic situation. Italy, Spain, Portugal, and Greece have all experienced a rapid demographic decrease and have thus ceased to offer a reserve of labour force for Northern Europe, as they did in the 1970s. The second reason is the gradual convergence of living standards in those Southern European countries compared with those of Northern Europe, which developed around the same time as European freedom of circulation was achieved. Freedom of circulation also created opportunities for circulation without settlement, a trend which similarly increased in Eastern European countries, when citizens of new EU Member States adopted mobility as a way of life between Romania, Poland, and Western European countries. For Eastern Europe after the 1990s, circular migration became possible as a result of the opening of borders thanks to their entry into the EU. Over the last 30 years, all Southern European countries, which were formerly emigration countries, became new immigration countries.

In countries on the southern rim of the Mediterranean Sea, the situation regarding the relationship between migration and development is different from in Southern European countries, as there is no prospect of them joining the EU and they do not benefit from European structural funds. The common trend of European countries granting more aid in exchange for a reduction in migration is essentially misguided. In particular, we must distinguish between the short-term and long-term consequences of such policies. In the long term we can presume that development (economic but also political), as well as demographic changes, will weaken the strongest pressures driving flows of low-skilled migration. However, in the short term, migration and development are mutually dependent. Development is a factor of migration and migration is a factor of development, because in the Global South migration is closely associated with modernity. Civil wars, terrorism, corruption, unemployment, and obstacles to human mobility all contribute to shaping the sociopolitical landscape. We must also distinguish between the different situations in the Maghreb, Turkey, and Sub-Saharan Africa. The Maghreb and Turkey have become places of transit and immigration, like Mexico, but they also have reserves of population and labour force. On the southern rim of the Mediterranean, 50% of the population is aged less than 25 years, and the median age in Sub-Saharan Africa is 19 years, compared with a median age of 41 years in Italy (it was 28 years in Italy in 1950). The rate of unemployment has reached 30% or even 40% in some countries, and young people therefore experience great difficulty in entering the labour market, either with or without higher qualifications. The difference in GNP between European countries and those of the southern Mediterranean rim can be as much as a factor of five. Development programs often lead to increased urbanisation, which also gives rise to both internal and external migration, owing to the abandonment of agriculture. In all these cases, then, we cannot assume that development will rapidly become an alternative to migration, as it was for Southern Europe in the 1960s and 1970s.

The relationship between development and migration has become a question of international relations, because development policy is considered as a tool of international migration policy, with the goal of reducing migration. This approach has been enshrined at the international level in international policy, mostly through bilateral agreements concerning repatriation, even though most research (for example, the findings produced by the Institut de recherche sur le développement and the Association française de développement) has shown that migration facilitates development and that development encourages migration. Remittances, agreements of co-development concluded between countries of origin and countries of immigration, and local development initiatives facilitated by transnational diasporas all continue to illustrate the role of development in relation to migration, and to demonstrate ways in which migration and development work together rather than being alternatives to one another.

In the twenty-first century, more than half of all migrants live in developed countries, and 28 countries receive 75% of the world's migrants. Europe and the US alone receive half of all migrants. Among migrants living in developed countries, 54% come from developing countries, while 80% of migrants living in developing countries come from other developing countries.

Over the last 30 years, the greatest number of development policies have targeted the Maghreb and Sub-Saharan Africa. Other major initiatives have been arranged between Germany and Turkey, and between Mexico and the US.

Several factors explain the rise of migration in places where certain gaps or inequalities can be observed: the demographic gap between poor and "young" countries in relation to rich and "old" countries, the role of mass media and other information and communication technologies in countries of departure in depicting a Western way of life, differences in salaries, remittances (now totalling $550 billion per year), the existence of transnational diasporas and cultural links, the presence of human smugglers offering to arrange passage, the rapid urbanisation of developing countries, an absence of hope in some contexts, and the environmental challenges, civil wars, and lack of security facing certain populations, mostly in the Global South. Both countries of arrival and countries of departure try to use migrants and their activities (remittances, elite diasporas, associations of co-development) as development tools in countries of origin. This so-called "win-win" strategy is increasingly being recognised and adopted, and development is increasingly being included in discussions of migration in the context of multilateral migration governance. In short, migration is increasingly being politically linked with development.

6.1   I – Development by Exile

Migration and mobility are becoming a factor of development in countries of departure. The UNDP 2009 Report declared that mobility had become the most important factor of human development. Migration improves standards of living and access to consumption, it reduces risks (economic, political, social, health) in unsafe countries of origin lacking health and social welfare, it brings remittances to families (which represent a total sum that is three times greater than all public development funds), and it grants some freedom and agency to individuals, as they become the main actors shaping their own future. However, migration can also create gaps between regions of emigration and regions without emigration. Most migrants do not consider returning to settle in their country of origin, and they prefer to send their money to their families rather than to the state, which they tend not to trust. Mobility develops transnational economic networks, decreases unemployment, exports social dissent, and allows those who remain in the place to live better lives and to benefit from the receipt of remittances.

Several development policies linked with migration have been implemented by EU Member States and the US since the 1970s. The earliest such policies were focused on the return of migrants to their countries of origin, such as those in Germany in relation to Turks since 1972, those in the Netherlands in relation to Moroccans since 1975, and those in France pertaining to all migrants, but especially to those from the Maghreb, since 1977. The slogan of "leaving in order to stay" ("partir pour rester") – that is, some members of a community emigrate in order to allow others to remain in place, possibly with the aim of themselves returning later – became popular in public policies. Funds were allocated to support migrants wishing to return to their country of origin (a policy associated with Lionel Stoleru, State Secretary for Immigration and Manual Work in France in 1977), and reinsertion programs aimed to help migrants to resettle with a productive economic activity. In France these reinsertion programs were implemented in 1981 (the French-Algerian agreement of return and reinsertion), in 1983 (involving a partnership between the state and large firms), and in 1998 (the Migration and Co-Development programme led by Sami Naïr). Few of these schemes were successful because they provided only short training programs, and also because most migrants intended to return to their country of origin only after retirement age, sometimes with the aim of then working as taxi drivers or shopkeepers and using their money to build a large home in their former villages, as a symbol of their successful emigration and return. Other obstacles to the success of these projects were migrants' lack of inclination to run businesses, their lack of previous training, the difficulties they faced with administration in their countries of origin, and sometimes corruption. The situation has still not changed substantially, since the profiles of returnees, their intentions, and their level of education and training still do not generally allow them to become managers of their own development. Most remittances are sent to migrants' families in order to improve their daily lives and to mitigate for the lack of insurance (health, environmental, or against political or economic risks) in countries where the future is insecure. Only relatively small sums of money are devoted to collective investments, because migrants have little trust in the governments of failed states.

6.1.1 *Constructing Development Between Non-state Actors*

In the 1980s, remittances were first considered as low-productivity investments, as they were directed towards ostentatious housing and consumption, or invested in coffee shops, grocery shops, or taxi businesses in rural and isolated regions of emigration, without any potential for economic development. However, it gradually became apparent that, in many countries of origin, remittances are the most substantial source of investment, ahead of public development funds, and that migrants abroad continue to send remittances even if they themselves do not intend to return. Public policies have therefore come to be focused on remittances.

A new strategy with an emphasis on co-development began to emerge in the mid-1990s. Faced with the relative failure of return policies, and informed by experts' findings regarding the mutual interdependence between migration and development in the short term (Tapinos, 1994), these policies – implemented in immigration countries in agreement with countries or regions of departure – focused on supporting migrants' initiatives directed towards their countries of origin through development associations, remittances, and transnational economic diasporas. The destination of funding is a crucial point, since, in the past, a significant proportion of public aid and subsidies has failed to reach the population, and has been used by governments for other purposes. The European Commission began to offer direct assistance to development associations in the Maghreb and Sub-Saharan Africa, such as the MEDA programs included in the Barcelona process (1995–2005), which are focused on collective projects of public interest and sustainable development (water, electrification, education, health, roads, rural tourism, urban housing programmes). Some projects of decentralised cooperation were undertaken between regions and large cities of the Global North (Europe) and the South (the Maghreb or

African cities), without the mediation of states. However, the scope of such initiatives remained limited and dependent on the mobility of actors. Although the long-term residence permits attained by some migrants allowed them to come and go freely, those who were repatriated lost their residence permits and subsequently required visas if they wished to return to Europe. The potential of these projects was weakened by the lack of expertise and empowerment on the part of associative migrant leaders in economic entrepreneurship and development, as well as by the tendency of development associations in countries of origin to become tools for advancing political careers (Lacroix, 2005).

Policies continue to focus on remittances as one of the main factors of development: immigration countries try to encourage remittances, for example through tax breaks on such transfers, while private companies such as Western Union facilitate the sending of remittances. Meanwhile, emigration countries encourage migrants to deposit funds related to remittances in banks, which helps to provide funds for long-term investments in collective projects. Some so-called "co-development policies" are the counterpart to bilateral or multilateral readmission agreements: if a country of origin accepts the responsibility to repatriate irregular migrants or failed asylum seekers, it will in return receive money for its development policies, as well as visas to allow the most qualified candidates to travel abroad. These agreements are often expressed in terms of sustainability and solidarity.

Meanwhile, the phenomenon of brain drain, which is another major topic of debate in North-South relations, has gradually come to be seen as a source of economic dynamism in the South, and part of a "win-win-win" approach: migration can become positive for migrants, for countries of immigration, and for countries of emigration. Some experts observe that one-fourth of doctors trained in Africa do not go on to practice medicine in Africa. Some European countries, such as the UK, Germany, and France have reopened their borders to high qualified workers from all over the world, in a context of strong competition to attract elites. These highly qualified workers from developing countries often have low chances of finding a job corresponding to their qualifications in their countries of origin, owing to unemployment and an absence of free competition in access to senior roles or facilities for entrepreneurship. However, qualified and highly qualified people send remittances to their countries of origin, maintain diasporic transnational networks, and contribute to development. In this context, an apparent "brain drain" can be transformed into a "brain gain" (through empowerment thanks to the provision of facilities to national investors abroad, and the development of sustainable projects with less bureaucracy). Through co-development programs, immigration can contribute to a sharing of resources rather than enlarging the gap between sending and receiving countries. However, the situation varies according to conditions in the countries of emigration: whereas in India or China, for example, the departure of highly qualified elites does not harm development, owing to the number of such elites and the facilities they have developed in order to build networks of qualified work in these countries of origin, for some small African countries with a strong emigration of elites the situation poses greater problems.

6.1.2 Migration Leads to Development

Migration is a factor of development. Remittances towards countries of origin continue to increase. They represented $280 billion in 2006, $337 billion in 2007, $328 billion in 2008, and have now reached the level of $550 billion (World Bank annual reports). Meanwhile, the amount of public aid devoted to development stands at only one-fourth of the level of remittances. These remittances represent 20% of GNP in Cape Verde and Senegal, and 10% in Mali, the Philippines (where one-tenth of inhabitants are migrants), and Morocco. In some countries, remittances are not transmitted through banks but through informal networks, such as in the "trabendo" (black market) in Algeria. Transnational networks (families, economic links, and cultural exchanges) contribute to co-development policies, leading to increased well-being in regions of departure. Migration also exports unemployment and social dissent, while offering the prospect of highly qualified jobs to migrants. Migrants can become actors of development in their regions of origin through initiatives of decentralised cooperation. Some historical analyses have shown that, in the past, cases where a large proportion of the population emigrated from Northern Europe countries led to an increase in living conditions for those who remained in place, owing to shortages of land for agriculture (Bade, 1994).

However, migration can also give rise to a relationship of dependency between regions of departure and countries of immigration, as a result of the flow of remittances. Several field studies show that families of migrants are less competitive in agriculture or businesses when they receive funds from abroad, and that immigration leads to brain drain. Migrants send funds to improve educational conditions for their children, to help their families to remain in place without moving to large cities or abroad, and to reduce poverty. Migration then becomes a strategy of adaptation and development in countries of low resources that have entered a transitional economic phase. For example, in the Philippines, "care drain" (the emigration of nurses or "badanti" to care for older people in Italy) is becoming a source of brain drain, as children trained in private schools leave the country to work abroad. Is there a real will to reduce migration in countries such as these? European policies that try to enlist African states in controlling irregular migration through the use of bilateral agreements may therefore be working at cross-purposes, if migration and remittances are the main factor of development for these countries, and for the wellbeing of the families of migrants. 69% of migrants in the world do not leave the Global South, and two-thirds of refugees are received by developing countries, sometimes poorer than their country of origin. It is therefore apparent that the forms of development promoted by remittances and bilateral agreements cannot prevent migration from taking place.

6.1.3 *Development Leads to Migration*

Inversely, development often gives rise to migration. The rapid modernisation of agriculture, accelerated by the global development projects of the International Monetary Fund or the World Bank, is producing a rural exodus, with populations moving first to the urban peripheries of large cities of the Global South, and then to international destinations. Many developing countries are now faced with a situation that resembles the situation of some European countries in the nineteenth century, when economic growth led to a rural exodus and massive urbanisation, and subsequently to large-scale emigration (for example, in Italy, Germany, Ireland, and the UK). Development can also lead to the emergence of dissent on the part of migrants towards their countries of origin, when the latter are undemocratic, corrupt, poor, or when they offer limited perspectives for either employment or political change. These conditions drive the most educated, informed, and cosmopolitan migrants to leave in order to succeed elsewhere, using migration as a tool to escape the limitations imposed by life in such countries. These elite migrants consider that, in their country of origin, they have no hope of achieving their goals, even though they are not among the poorest inhabitants. The urbanisation of developing countries leads to an increase in migration, owing to the increased access to information and transportation.

Finally, countries of departure generally consider the departure of their own nationals as a positive factor for themselves and their societies, whereas immigration countries generally consider immigrants as a negative factor for their societies.

Other initiatives, inspired by the North American Free Trade Agreement (NAFTA) between the US, Canada, and Mexico, have tried to bring about a mobility of trade without allowing for the mobility of people, but these measures have had limited success in decreasing migration, such as between Mexico and the US (which is inhabited by 12 million irregular migrants). The Euro Mediterranean programs (MEDA), integrated in the Barcelona Program (1995–2005), used the same approach, with an emphasis on improving infrastructure for the transmission of remittances (encouraging the use of banks and promoting micro-projects). These measures aimed to facilitate a direct exchange between migrants as senders and their families as receivers, without the mediation of states or institutions. They also encouraged programs of collective interest and decentralised co-development, relating, for example, to water, electricity, roads, and rural tourism. In France, Moroccans, Malians, and Senegalese are the nationalities who have invested the most in migrant development associations, some of which also receive funds from the EU. Migrants' projects tend to be local, sometimes communitarian (for example, in the case of the Murids, a Senegalese group in the region of Tuba), and are rarely orientated towards national aims. Overall, these projects are limited in scope, and do not have an impact on broad patterns of migration. Most migrants are drawn to Europe, not by demographic pressures or extreme poverty, but by the desire to change their own life and to escape from their countries of origin, even if the border-crossing journey may lead to their death. This is why development or co-development cannot be considered a solution to stopping migration, and why migration is not the unique solution to the challenges of development. Whereas migration dynamics provide a short-term solution, development is a medium- or long-term process.

6.1.4 Highly Differentiated Situations Across the World

The impact of migration on development and of development on migration differs not only in their respective short-term and long-term perspectives, but also according to the profiles of the countries of departure. In the US, the role of Latin American migrant associations on development in the country of origin was analysed by Alejandro Portes and Cristina Escobar (Princeton University). They conducted comparative field studies between several countries of Latin America, focused on the use of remittances and on the efficiency of the so-called "Tres por Uno" program (whereby, when a migrant in the US sends one dollar to their family, the government of the country of origin grants another two dollars, at either the national or local level). Their findings revealed a diversity of situations across these countries of departure.

They showed that projects led by migrants changed the way that migrants were viewed in their own countries of origin. Whereas they had formerly been viewed as having run away, or even as being traitors, their image improved thanks to their sending of remittances. Mexicans, Colombians, and Dominicans created transnational associations with their regions of departure. Their degree of success was linked to their trust in the state in their country of origin, the existence of a tradition of partnership with civil society, and with the particular profiles of migrants belonging to the three nationalities, as well as the types of projects undertaken and the tools that were used to implement them. Mexican development associations performed the best, as they continued to work with the state for more than 10 years in the "Tres por Uno" program. In the Colombian case, projects were more independent from the state, and in the Dominican case projects were transnational.

In Sub-Saharan Africa, remittances constitute an effective tool in the fight against poverty, but also more broadly in addressing the uncertainty of the future, in the face of risks of illness, civil wars, unemployment, family disruption, and environmental crisis. Remittances are thus mainly used as a form of insurance against such risks. Countries that have developed a strong dependency on remittances, such as Burkina Faso, are intrinsically fragile. In Mali, Mauritania, and Senegal, many local activities have been initiated thanks to immigrant associations that send remittances for collective purposes (international migrant solidarity organisations), such as programmes devoted to health, education, water, and electricity. In these countries, remittances are rarely invested in developing productive activities, owing to an unfavourable environment for such investments (a lack of trust towards administration and mediators, political instability, and the weakness of structures involved in providing micro-credit). More often, migration leads to further migration, but is not an alternative to development. Only an easier circulation of people between emigration and immigration countries is likely to support the continued success of such projects.

Morocco became a country of immigration while remaining a country of departure. Many initiatives of co-development were undertaken (Lacroix, 2005): return-reinsertion policies, banking infrastructure for remittances, the relocation of activities that required considerable amounts of labour, aid for projects of delocalised cooperation, direct foreign investment, and the pursuit of free trade as an alternative to migration. None of these initiatives produced significant results because the individual decision to migrate is often very far removed from the development policies of the country of departure, as well as from the aims of countries of immigration that wish to stop irregular migration and satisfy anti-migrant public opinion. Unemployment has given rise to the mobility of both qualified and unqualified migrants, and the subsequent existences of diasporas, which have then given rise to development associations.

In China, the rise of economic liberalism went hand in hand with the construction of new relations with Western countries, largely as a result of migration. The deregulation of the labour market in China, along with the "hukou" system dividing the population between rural and urban contexts and limiting internal migration from the countryside to cities, created a new underclass which was attracted by the prospect of informal employment in Western countries. This migration also created a significant diaspora. The professionalization of emigration from China also gradually led to Chinese migrants overseas taking jobs that were not related to their migratory origin. The distinction between desired and undesired migration remains very ambiguous in China.

In many countries of the Global South, elite Diasporas of knowledge are closely connected with development. In the mid-1970s, many researchers from Southern countries considered brain drain to be harmful to the development of countries of departure. Now, however, most research is in favour of the "diaspora option": that is, the hypothesis that the migration of human capital may have a beneficial effect on economic development and on the level of education in countries of origin. This allows them to produce a more highly qualified labour force, and also to be viewed more positively abroad. South Korea, Colombia, India, and China are all engaged in developing these sorts of elite networks. However, the "diaspora option", as a tool of development, often only complements existing dynamics of knowledge transfer. The development of information and communication technologies in India shows that social networks allow a better management of information and promote scientific activity in the country of origin, thereby increasing productivity. The paradigm of global circulation has therefore come to replace the model of brain drain.

6.1.5 The Win-Win-Win Approach

The strategy of directing international aid towards development goals and the sending of remittances may help to locate sources of subsidies for health and education. The impact of remittances is unequal because those who are able to leave a country of departure are generally not among the poorest inhabitants. Aid generally has a positive effect on indicators of human development, but it may also have a negative effect in cases where it leads to a relationship of dependency. There are winners and losers among countries who receive aid. In the Mediterranean region, migrants from Algeria, Morocco, Tunisia, and Turkey send remittances on a smaller scale than migrants from Sub-Saharan Africa, because there are weaker reasons driving them to transfer money. The profile of the type of migrant who sends the largest remittances is that of an older migrant, who owned a house in their country of origin, and arrived in Europe in the 1970s. The migrant's attachment to their country is very important. More recent waves of migrants are sending less money, with a diversification according to the country of immigration in question. Those settled in Quebec send less than those settled in Europe (El Mouhoub, 2017).

6.2 Conclusion

The relationship between migration and development is a common topic in all global approaches to migration, in the programs of NGOs and IGOs, as well as in regional summits and bilateral and multilateral agreements. However, while development is an important concern in itself, it has never been a viable solution to reducing migration. All international research built on field research shows that it has no impact on migration in the short term, and that stopping migration would also stop human development, as the COVID-19 crisis showed in 2020. The success of this topic is perhaps linked with the Christian cultures of Northern countries and their attitudes towards developing countries, together with political discourses that suggest that immigration countries could reduce or even stop migration by pursuing development goals, even though this does not happen in practice. This does not mean, however, that we should abandon development work; it is worth pursuing, quite apart from the goal of reducing migration.

References

Bade, K. (1994). *L'Europe en mouvement. la migration de la fin du XVII ème siècle à nos jours.* paris, Seuil, 2002.

El Mouhoub, M. (2017). *L'immigration en France: Mythes et réalités.* Fayard.

Lacroix, T. (2005). *Les réseaux marocains du développement: Géographie du transnational et politiques du territorial.* Presses de Sciences Po.

Tapinos, G. (1994). *Migrations et développement.* OECD report.

Open Access This chapter is licensed under the terms of the Creative Commons Attribution 4.0 International License (http://creativecommons.org/licenses/by/4.0/), which permits use, sharing, adaptation, distribution and reproduction in any medium or format, as long as you give appropriate credit to the original author(s) and the source, provide a link to the Creative Commons license and indicate if changes were made.

The images or other third party material in this chapter are included in the chapter's Creative Commons license, unless indicated otherwise in a credit line to the material. If material is not included in the chapter's Creative Commons license and your intended use is not permitted by statutory regulation or exceeds the permitted use, you will need to obtain permission directly from the copyright holder.

Conclusion of the Book

The various relations and interdependencies between migration and international relations have led us to examine the diversity of structures (nation states, IGOs, NGOs, etc.), actors (migrants and refugees, citizens, and foreigners), and forms of contact (migration diplomacy, multilateral governance) that are involved, from the local to the global level. The globalisation of migration and its rising place in political discourses, along with the continuing poor management of migration and the difficulty of convincing public opinion that migration is a structural and interdependent phenomenon at the international level, all help to explain why this topic is still important today. This book attempts to explain the main developments in the field, with an analysis of the main concepts and controversies, a historical overview, and a geographical coverage mainly focused on Europe.

It may be useful to summarise here the claims and premises of each chapter. Chapter One explains the nature of migration as a globalised, structural, and interdependent phenomenon across the world, since this crucially makes it an international issue which cannot be solved at the national level. The history of migration policies, discussed in Chapter Two, shows that migration played a central role in the creation of the modern world, even if many people did not move from their place of origin, and were sometimes prohibited to do so, notably in the case of slaves and feudal serfs, and in periods where a large population was a symbol of wealth and required for the purposes of war, taxation, and agriculture. Today the international visa system creates a hierarchy between those who are allowed to move and those who are not, which is polarised across the North/South divide and between the rich and the poor. Northern immigration countries define the rules of migration at the world level, using security-based approaches, even though the conclusions of efforts towards establishing a multilateral governance of migration recommend a greater opening of borders to allow through more legal migrants, for work, but also for demographic reasons and in order to respect human rights. Chapter Three, on the subject of the "refugee crisis", analyses both older and more recent trends from the last thirty years, which broadly involve the use of refugee policies to reinforce security-based policies of immigration control, thereby undermining the rights of asylum seekers. It also underlines the need to harmonise access to refugee status, and to provide greater transparency in the criteria used to grant refugee status. In order to extend the limits of citizenship (Chapter Four), a more inclusive model of citizenship is required, which would provide access to local political rights for all resident foreigners, as well as easier access to citizenship based either on settlement or on the place of birth (*jus soli*). Meanwhile, negotiations around dual citizenship between countries of origin and immigration countries would build bridges and help to integrate immigrants. This chapter emphasises the need to fight against processes that lead to irregular migrants remaining in this vulnerable state in the long term, and that tolerate the status quo regarding stateless people and other forms of denying citizenship. Chapter Five, devoted to migration diplomacy, presents the issue of migration in the international arena. Its emergence as a topic of debate has brought new legitimacy to this issue, which was formerly despised and neglected as a topic of international relations, but the ethos of multiculturalism is still not widely accepted in this field, and this diplomacy requires more transparency. As Chapter Six explains, the relations between migration and development give rise to many misunderstandings, although they are closely related, both in their short-term and medium-term horizons. Most of these conclusions, although fundamental, still need to be explained, because migration studies is a relatively new field in the domain of research in international relations.

However, in a context that features not only a growing body of knowledge, but also the growth of populism built on the hatred of migration, diversity, and multiculturalism, what can research do?

Max Weber's essays "Science as a Vocation" and "Politics as a Vocation" (1919) distinguishes between value-based, action-orientated, and evidence-based or truth-orientated frameworks for understanding the normative architecture and social practices of science and politics. In light of Weber's conclusions, the tension between, on the one hand, the dynamics of truth and scientific logic and, on the other hand, the conflicts of values or interests, the quest for power, and the security agenda that prevails in Europe, remain crucial in the policy-making debate today.

The politicisation of migration issues remains acute in the current context of extreme political tensions: populist parties' electoral successes are built on the use of xenophobic themes and anti-immigration rhetoric, and have also taken place against the backdrop of humanitarian crises at the borders of Europe and the social consequences of the economic crisis. The politicisation of migration and the use of scientific and expert knowledge in the EU are key factors in the current migration regime.

Europe is currently facing a "migration crisis", which constitutes a significant challenge. However, attempts to "manage" the crisis, both on the part of individual Member States and of the EU collectively, through security-orientated and anti-immigration policy instruments, seem to produce ever greater controversies and limited results. As a measure of the "success" of such measures, we need only consider the thousands of deaths that have occurred in the Mediterranean Sea, the creation of both formal and informal camps, the emergence of tensions on the borders of Europe, the violation of rights and legal provisions at the national, European, and international level, and the proliferation of human smuggling and trafficking and other criminal activities connected to migration and migrants.

The gap between expert knowledge on migration and the representations of migration used in policy-making arenas constitutes another gap with regard to migration and refugee policies in the EU. Why do policymakers adhere to decisions and policy options that have demonstrably failed to achieve their stated goals in the past? The answer can be found in the inability of nation states, with a focus on borders and sovereignty, to rise to the challenges of the inherently global phenomenon of migration and refugees, as well as the role of public opinion in influencing the decision-making process, which leads decision-makers to show a lack of interest in human rights and ethics in this field, and a short-term preference for path-dependent approaches at the international level.

Bibliography

Agier, M. (2014). *Un monde de camps*. La découverte.
Agier, M. (2019). *L'étranger qui vient*. Gallimard.
Akoka, K. (2020). *L'asile et l'exil*. La découverte.
Ambrosini, M., Cinalli, M., & Jacobson, D. (Eds.). (2020). *Migration, borders and citizenship: Between policy and public spheres*. Palgrave Macmillan.
Bade, K. (1994). *L'Europe en mouvement. la migration de la fin du XVII ème siècle à nos jours*. paris, Seuil, 2002.
Bade, K. (2002). *L'Europe en mouvement: La migration de la fin du XVIIIème siècle à nos jours*. Seuil.
Badie, B. (2009). *Puissant ou solidaire? Principes d'humanisme international*. Desclée de Bouwer.
Badie, B. (2022, November 16–17). Conference. Grenoble Institute of Political Studies.
Badie, B., Brauman, R., Decaux, E., Devin, G., & Wihtol de Wenden, C. (2008). *Pour un autre regard sur les migrations: Construire une gouvernance globale*. La découverte.
Baillat, A. (2015). *The soft diplomacy of poor nation states: Bangladesh involved in environmental risks* [Doctoral thesis, Sciences Po].
Balleix, C. (2022). *Enjeux et défis de la politique migratoire européenne*. Dalloz.
Basch, L., Glick-Schiller, N., & Szanton-Blanc, C. (1994). *Nations unbound: Transnational projects, post-colonial predicaments and de-territorialised nation states*. Routledge.
Bassi, M. (2015). Politiques de contrôle et gestion des réalités locales dans la gestion des migrations indésirables en Sicile. In C. Schmoll, H. Thiollet, & C. Wihtol de Wenden (Eds.), *Migrations en Méditerranée* (pp. 157–167). CNRS Editions.
Bauböck, R. (1994). *Transnational citizenship: Membership and rights in international migration*. Edward Elgar.
Bauböck, R. (2006). Towards a political theory of migrant transnationalism. *International Migration Review, 37*, 700–723.
Bauman, Z. (2000). *Liquid modernity*. Cambridge University Press.
Bertossi, C., & Wihtol de Wenden, C. (2007). *Les couleurs du drapeau: L'armée française face aux discriminations*. Robert Laffont.
Bigo, D., & Guild, E. (2005). *Controlling frontiers: Free movement into or within Europe*. Ashgate.
Black, R. (2001). Fifty years of refugee studies: From theory to policy. *International Migration Review, 35*, 57.
Body-Gendrot, S., & Wihtol de Wenden, C. (2014). *Policing the inner cities in France, the United Kingdom and the United States*. Palgrave/Pivot.
Bretell, C., & Hollifield, J. (2014). *Migration theory: Talking across disciplines*. Routledge.
Brubaker, R. (1992). *Citizenship and nationhood in France and Germany*. Harvard University Press.

Brubaker, R. (2000). *Citoyenneté et nationalité en France et en Allemagne*. Belin.
Caponio, T. (2022). Scaling migration network governance? City networks and civil society in multilevel policymaking dynamics. *Global Networks, 22*, 397–412. https://doi.org/10.1111/glob.12365
Castles, S. (1997). Multicultural citizenship: A response to the dilemma of globalisation and national identity. *Journal of Intercultural Studies, 18*(1), 5–23.
Castles, S. (2017). *Migration, citizenship and identity*. Edward Elgar.
Castles, S., & Davidson, A. (2000). *Citizenship and migration: Globalisation and the politics of belonging*. Macmillan.
Castles, S., De Haas, H., & Miller, M. (2014). *The age of migration: International movements of population in the modern world*. Macmillan.
Cesari, J. (1994). *Être musulman en France*. Karthala.
Cohen, R. (2008). *Global diasporas, an introduction*. Routledge.
Cohen, R. (2021). *Migration: The movement of humankind from prehistory to the present*. André Deutsch.
Comte, E. (2018). *The history of the European migration regime: Germany's strategic hegemony*. Routledge.
Cornelius, W., & Hollifield, J. (Eds.). (1996). *Migration between states and markets*. Oxford University Press.
Cornelius, W., Hollifield, J., & Martin, P. (Eds.). (1994). *Controlling migration: A global perspective*. Stanford University Press.
de Gutcheneire, P., Pécoud, A., & Cholewski, R. (2009). *Migration and human rights: The UN Convention of Migrants*. UNESCO and Cambridge University Press.
De Haas, H. (2010). Migration and development: A theoretical perspective. *International Migration Review, 44*(1), 227–264.
Dufoix, S. (2003). *Les diasporas*. Presses Universitaires de France.
El Mouhoub, M. (2017). *L'immigration en France: Mythes et réalités*. Fayard.
Entzinger, H. (2006). Changing the rules when the game is on: From multiculturalism in the Netherlands. In M. Bodemann & G. Yundaku (Eds.), *Migration, citizenship, ethnos: Incorporation regimes in Germany, Western Europe and North America*. Palgrave Macmillan.
Etienne, B. (1989). *La France et l'Islam*. Hachette.
European Commission. (2001). *European governance: A white paper, Brussels 25/7/2001 COM(2001) 428 final*. European Commission.
Faist, T. (2019). *The transnational social question*. Oxford University Press.
Feld, S. (2019). *Les migrations internationales et le développement*. L'Harmattan.
Foucher, M. (2007). *L'obsession des frontières*. Perrin.
Garces-Mascarenas, B., & Penninx, R. (2015). *Integration processes and policies in Europe* (IMISCOE research series). Springer.
Gedo, E., & Szenasi, E. (Eds.). (2022). *Populism and migration*. L'Harmattan.
Gemenne, F., Ionesco, D., & Mokhachevna, D. (2016). *Atlas des migrations environnementales*. Presses de Sciences Po.
Granovetter, M. (1973). The strength of weak ties. *American Journal of Sociology, 78*(6), 1360–1380.
Green, T. (2020). *The Covid consensus: The new politics of global inequalities*. Hurst.
Grimmel, A., & Giang, S. M. (Eds.). (2017). *Solidarity in the European Union*. Springer.
Haddad, E. (2008). *The refugee in international society: Between sovereigns*. Cambridge University Press.
Hammar, T. (1990). *Democracy and the nation state: Aliens, denizens, and citizens in a world of international migration*. Avebury.
Hinger, S. (2021). Paper at conference at CERI organised by Thomas Lacroix on "Cities and Migration", 10/9/2021.
Hirschman, A. (1970). *Exit, voice and loyalty: Responses to decline in firms, organisations and states*. Harvard University Press.

Hollifield, J. (1992). *Immigration, markets and states: American policy and politics*. Harvard University Press.
Hollifield, J. (1998–1999). Migration, trade and the nation state: The myth of globalisation. *UCLA Journal of International Law and Foreign Affairs, 3*, 585–636.
Hollifield, J. (2021). Driven out: Displacement and the challenge of forced migration. *The Wilson Quarterly, 3* (special issue: Humanity in motion: Scenes from the global displacement crisis).
Hollifield, J., & Brettell, I. (2022). *Migration theory: Talking across disciplines*. Routledge.
Hollifield, J., Martin, P., Orrenius, P., & Heran, F. (Eds.). (2022). *Controlling immigration: A comparative perspective*. Stanford University Press.
Huntington, S. (1993). The clash of civilisations. *Foreign Affairs, 72*(3), 22–49.
Huntington, S. (2004). *Qui sommes-nous? Identité nationale et choc des cultures*.
Infantino, F., & Sredanovic, D. (Eds.). (2022). *Migration control in practice: Before and within the borders of the state*. Éditions de l'Université de Bruxelles.
Kant, I. (2006). *Projet de paix perpétuelle*. Nathan.
Kepel, G. (1987). *Les banlieues de l'Islam*. Le Seuil.
Koser, K. (2007). Refugees, transnationalism and the state. *Journal of Ethnic and Migration Studies, 33*, 233–254.
Kymlicka, W. (1995). *Multicultural citizenship: A liberal theory of minority rights*. Oxford University Press.
Lacroix, T. (2005). *Les réseaux marocains du développement: Géographie du transnational et politiques du territorial*. Presses de Sciences Po.
Lacroix, T., & Spencer, S. (Eds.). (2022). Special issue: Cities in networks. *Global networks* (Vol. 22, issue 3).
Lavisse, E. (2014). *Histoire de France*. Armand Colin.
Le Blanc, G., & Brugère, F. (2017). *La fin de l'hospitalité: Lampedusa, Lesbos, Calais*. Flammarion.
Leveau, R., & Mohsen, K. (Eds.). (2005). *Musulmans de France et d'Europe*. CNRS Editions.
Leveau, R., & Wihtol de Wenden, C. (2001). *La beurgeoisie: Les trois âges de la vie associative issue de l'immigration*. CNRS Editions.
Levitt, P., & Jaworsky, N. (2007). Transnational migration studies: Past developments and future trends. *Annual Review of Sociology, 33*, 129–156.
Martiniello, M., & Rath, J. (Eds.). (2010). *Selected studies in international migration and immigrant incorporation*. Amsterdam University Press.
Massey, D. (2003). A synthetic theory of international migration. In *World in the mirror of international migration* (pp. 138–161). Max Press.
Massey, D. (2008). *New faces in new places: The changing geography of American immigration*. Russell/Sage.
Massey, D., Arango, J., & Taylor, E. (2005). *Words in motion: Understanding international migration at the end of the millennium*. Oxford University Press.
OECD, SOPEMI. (2020). *Perspectives on international migrations* (Annual report 2020).
Pécoud, A., & de Gutcheneire, P. (2007). *Migration without borders: Essays on the free movement of people*. UNESCO and Berghahn Books.
Pécoud, A., & de Gutcheneire, P. (2011). *Migration and climate change*. UNESCO and Cambridge University Press.
Pécoud, A., de Gutcheneire, P., & Cholewski, R. (2009). *Migration and human rights: The UN Convention of Migrants*. UNESCO and Cambridge University Press.
Pian, A. (2009). *Aux nouvelles frontières de l'Europe: L'aventure incertaine des Sénégalais au Maroc*. La dispute.
Portes, A. (2003). Theoretical convergences and empirical evidence in the study of immigrant transnationalism. *International Migration Review, 37*, 814–892.
Portes, A., & Fernandez-Kelly, P. (Eds.). (2015). *The state and the grass roots: Immigrant transnational organisations in four countries*. Berghahn Books.
Price, M. (2009). *Rethinking asylum: History, purpose and limits*. Cambridge University Press.
Rex, J., & Singh, G. (Eds.). (2004). *The governance of multiculturalism*. Ashgate.

Rodier, C. (2019). L'équation lucrative du contrôle des frontières. *L'Economie Politique: Alternatives Économiques, 84.* https://www.alternatives-economiques.fr/lequation-lucrative-controle-frontieres/00090972

Rosenau, J. (1990). *Turbulence in world politics.* Princeton University Press.

Safran, W. (1991). Diasporas in modern societies: Myths of homeland and return. *Diaspora, 1*(1), 83–99.

Sassen, S. (1996a). *La Ville globale.* Descartes et Cie.

Sassen, S. (1996b). *Losing control? Sovereignty in an age of globalisation.* Columbia University Press.

Sassen, S. (2014). *Expulsions: Brutality and complexity in the global economy.* Belknap Press.

Sayad, A. (1999). *La double absence.* Seuil.

Schain, M. (2008). *The politics of immigration in France, Britain and the United States: A comparative study.* Palgrave Macmillan.

Scheffer, G. (2006). *Diaspora politics: At home abroad.* Cambridge University Press.

Schierup, C.-U., Hansen, T., & Castles, S. (Eds.). (2007). *Migration, citizenship and the welfare state: A European dilemma.* Oxford University Press.

Schmoll, C., Thiollet, H., & Wihtol de Wenden, C. (2015). *Migrations en Méditerranée.* CNRS Editions.

Scholten, P. (2015). *Integrating immigrants in Europe* (IMISCOE research series). Springer.

Smith, S. (2018). *La ruée vers l'Europe.* Grasset.

Soysal, Y. (1994). *The limits of citizenship: Migrants and post-colonial citizenship in Europe.* Chicago University Press.

Tapinos, G. (1994). *Migrations et développement.* OECD report.

Tarrius, A. (2010). *Migrants internationaux et nouveaux réseaux criminels.* Trabucaire.

Thiesse, A.-M. (2006). National identities. In A. Dieckhoff & C. Jaffrelot (Eds.), *Revisiting nationalism: Theories and processes.* Hurst.

Thiollet, H. (2011). Migration as diplomacy: Labour, migrants, refugees and Arab regional politics in the oil rich countries. *International Labour and Working-Class History, 79,* 103–121.

Thouez, C. (2022). New power configurations: City mobilization and policy change. *Global Networks, 22*(3), 363–376.

Thranhardt, Dietrich, & Bommes, Michael. (2010). *National paradigms of migration research.* Osnabrück/IMIS/Universitäts Verlag.

UNDESA Report. (2021). *UNDESA International migration report 2021.*

UNHCR. (2022). *The state of the World refugees.*

Vasta, E., & Vuddamalay, V. (Eds.). (2006). *International migration and the social sciences.* Palgrave Macmillan.

Vertovec, S. (2004). Migrant transnationalism and modes of transformation. *International Migration Review, 38,* 970–2001.

Waldinger, R. (2004). Transnationalism in question. *American Journal of Sociology, 109*(5), 1117–1195.

Weil, P. (1989). *La France et ses étrangers 1945-1975.* Calmann-Lévy.

Weil, P. (2004). *Qu'est-ce qu'un Français? Histoire de la nationalité française depuis la Révolution.* Gallimard.

Weiner, M. (1995). *The global migration crisis: Challenges to states and to human rights.* Harper and Collins.

Wieviorka, M. (1994). *Racisme et xénophobie en Europe: Une comparaison internationale.* La découverte.

Wihtol de Wenden, C. (1988). *Les immigrés et la politique: Cent-cinquante ans d'évolution.* Presses de la FNSP.

Wihtol de Wenden, C. (1997). *La Citoyenneté européenne.* Presses de Sciences Po.

Wihtol de Wenden, C. (2004). Multiculturalism in France. In J. Rex & G. Singh (Eds.), *The governance of multiculturalism.* Ashgate.

Wihtol de Wenden, C. (2013). *Le droit d'émigrer.* CNRS Editions.

Wihtol de Wenden, C. (2017a). *La question migratoire au XXIème siècle: Migrants, réfugiés et relations internationales*. Presses de Sciences Po.
Wihtol de Wenden, C. (2017b). *Faut-il ouvrir les frontières?* Presses de Sciences Po.
Wihtol de Wenden, C. (2018). Knowledge and power: The impossible encounter. *Esprit, 7*, 183–189.
Wihtol de Wenden, C. (2019). Le pacte de Marrakech. In O. de Frouville (Ed.), *Vers un droit global*. Pedone.
Wihtol de Wenden, C. (2021). *Atlas des migrations*. Autrement.
Wihtol de Wenden, C. (2022a). Migrations méditerranéennes. *Pouvoirs, 183*, 87–97.
Wihtol de Wenden, C. (2022b). *Migrations: Un équilibre mondial à inventer*. Institut Diderot.
Zapata-Barrero, R., Caponio, T., & Scholten, P. (2017). Theorizing the local turn in a multi-level governance framework of analysis: A case study in immigrant policies. *International Review of Administrative Sciences, 83*(2), 241–246.
Zolberg, A. (1978). International policies in a changing world system. In W. McNeill & R. Adams (Eds.), *Human migrations: Patterns and policies* (pp. 5–27). Indiana University Press.
Zolberg, A. (1985). L'influence des facteurs externes sur l'ordre politique interne. In J. L. Jean & M. Grawitz (Eds.), *Traité de science politique*. Presses Universitaires de France.
Zolberg, A. (2006). *A nation by design: Immigration policy and the fashioning of America*. Cambridge University Press.
Zolberg, A., Suhrke, A., & Aguayo, S. (1989). *Escape from violence: Conflict and the refugee crisis in the developing world*. Oxford University Press.

Made in the USA
Monee, IL
03 May 2026